AF413705

A Deception Garden

by: Abigail K. Lloyd

DEDICATION

This book is dedicated to my teenage self.
You always deserved to express yourself in
a safe space.

CONTENTS

pyramid

disintegration hammers
          on the rusted metal roof;
resembling the hues of a blue tick hound;
it wears it—down
like
a hat;
waiting for the storms to buckle the seams;
they appear in the distance

stacked three eyes high

                         a pyramid
                          the sun
                        the ocean floor
in that order—for fun;

while I sit barefoot
and slovenly slack-jawed, watching
—tight fisting a water jug,
my anger turned apathetic,
waiting for the storm to turn

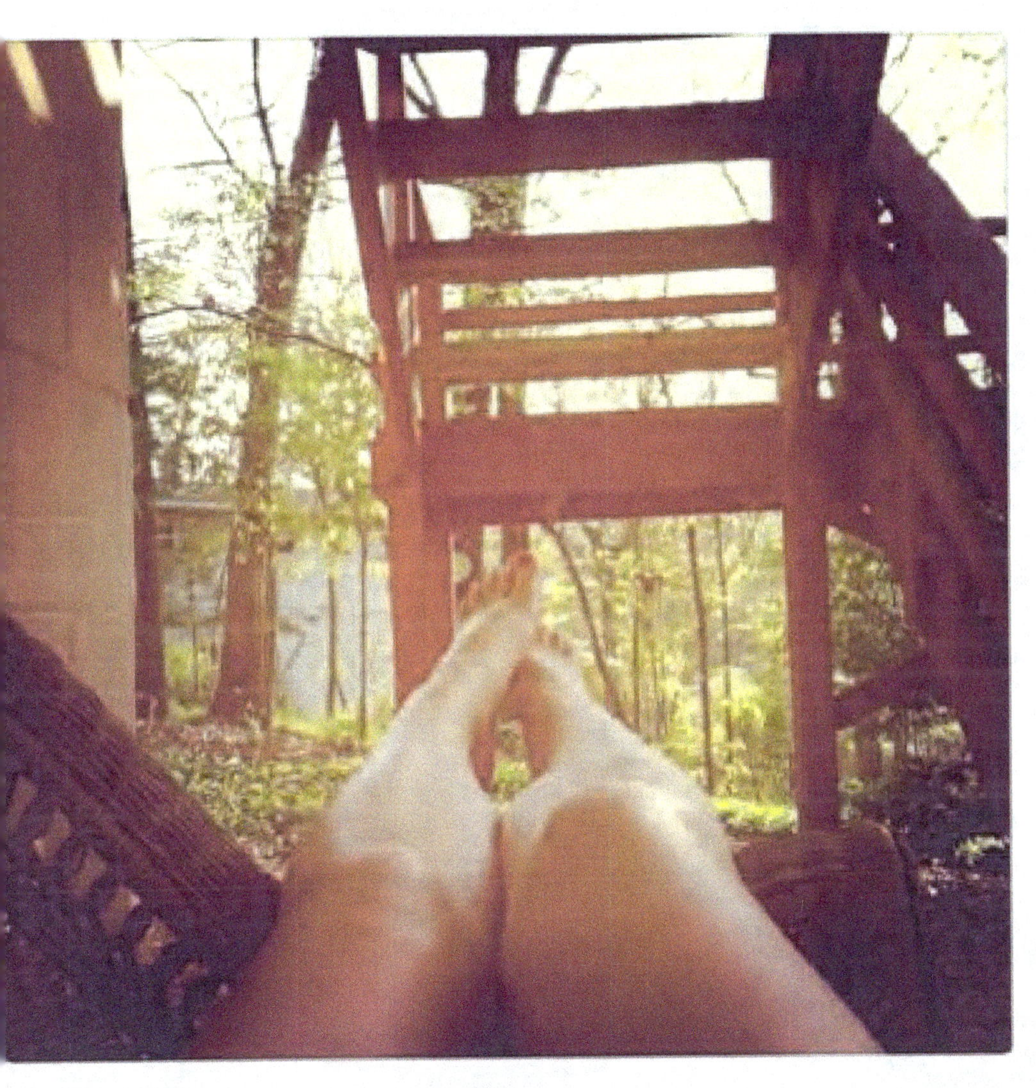

my legs [72714] Mar 27, 2012

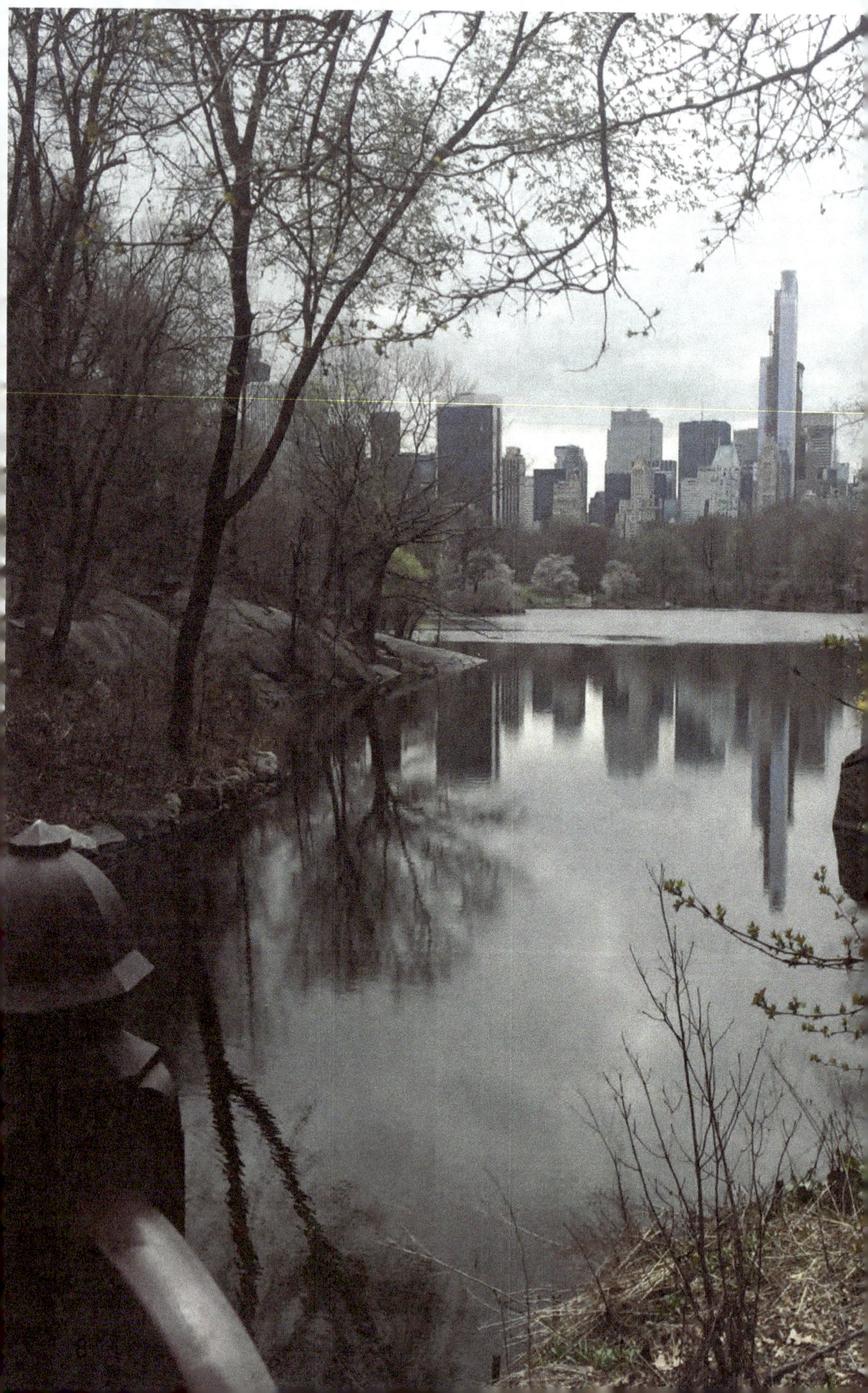

shallow

this room is crowded
     crammed from frayed paint
                    clippings
washing the floor full of debris;

I wish you could have gotten here faster—before
the ink embeds to lullabies,

breath paused, before
nightstands sitting with water ellipticals;

your breath is shallow,
        your grave—is deep;

deeper than lily pads invading a pond
        fond of frogs
        of nightfall
    of shadows creeping up from frost;

that rest on, the tip of my nose
while I gather your stones,
    stack them   one by   one
to line the bedframe,
under toe

present

There are days
when being present with my thoughts seem
pleasant—like I am in control—
like I didn't just manifest that
                        praying mantis
to keep
     me company

                    on my hammock swing.

  there are days
when a nervous breakdown keeps knocking
on my door;
                        "let me in," it says
                        "why?" I ask
                        "so I can tell you
          what I'll do to you
          when I get in." it says
I am the mom now, and I know
--there will be days like this—where
you can't get out of bed, where
words you've spoken like spells to people
are eating away at you like acid rain—which
they say,
"is inevitable this day and age"

you are mindful,
       you tell your brain
--you chose the wise path when your head
is pulling you to the left
and your heart to the right
which sometimes makes you feel
like you are being torn apart.

Your torn flesh suit suits you well
as we all walk as one in life—the idea that
     I am you
     and you are me
     and we are created in the image of
gods
     and gods cannot wear flesh suits
     I suppose

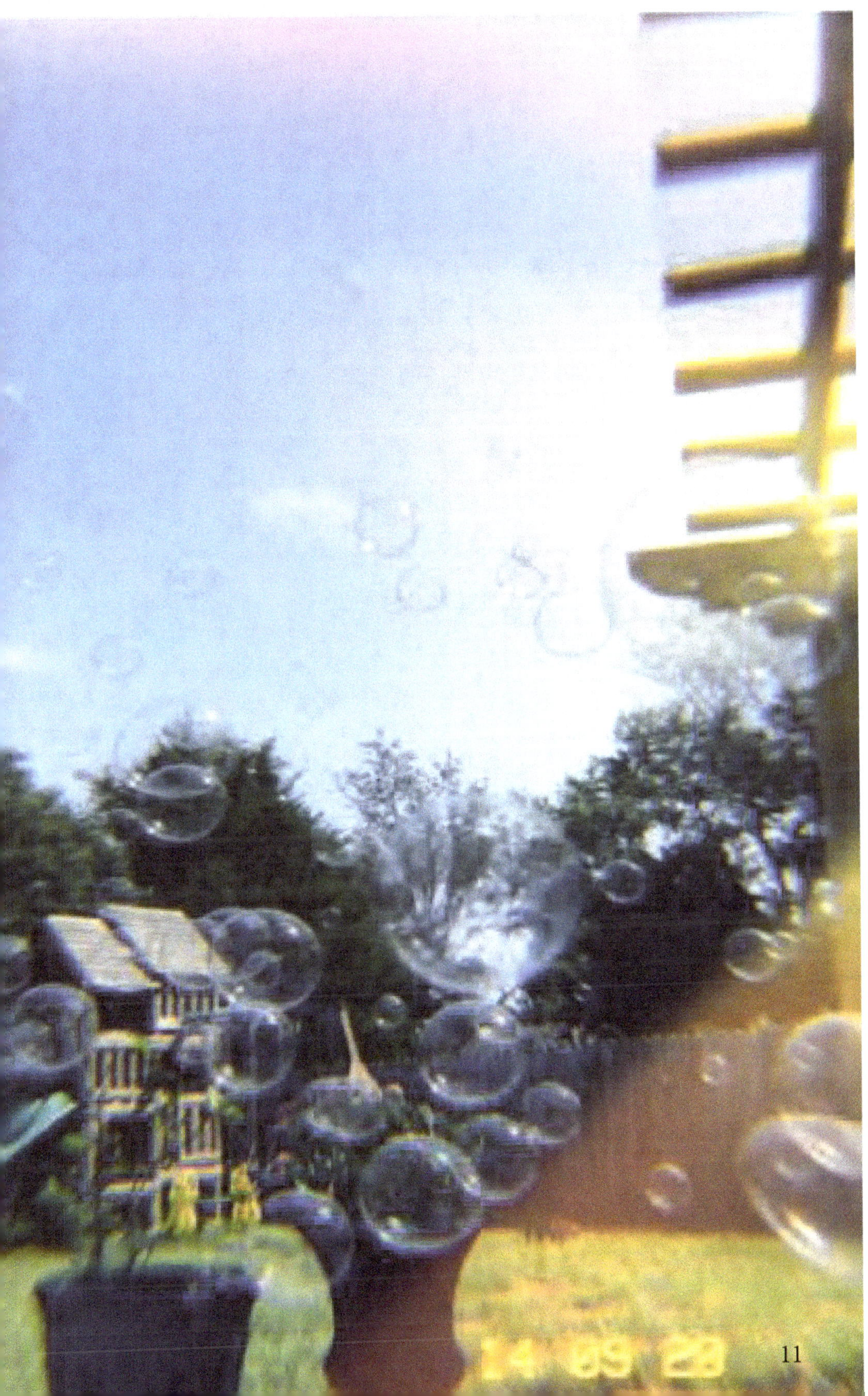
14 09 28

island

people talk of peace as if they have held it in their
hand—
fingers dragging dirt across separate leaves of grass,
the building of a soft paramount
sitting on a moss-covered chair—listening to
the trees   breathe;

my peace,
is piecing together parts of you
where you've told a lie;
a fragmented register of reality built from apprehended
soil, suspended over water;
that peace—murders me.

hungry at the back of my neck—collapses around my
throat—feeding my need
to scream.
so I sit;
soft canvas arms
draped across my knees
while sting rays wrap around the bottom of the boat—wax-
ing holes;

 to filter up water into air

waiting for me

to breathe

[blackslee waterfall walk, Enniskillen,
Ireland; August 2014]

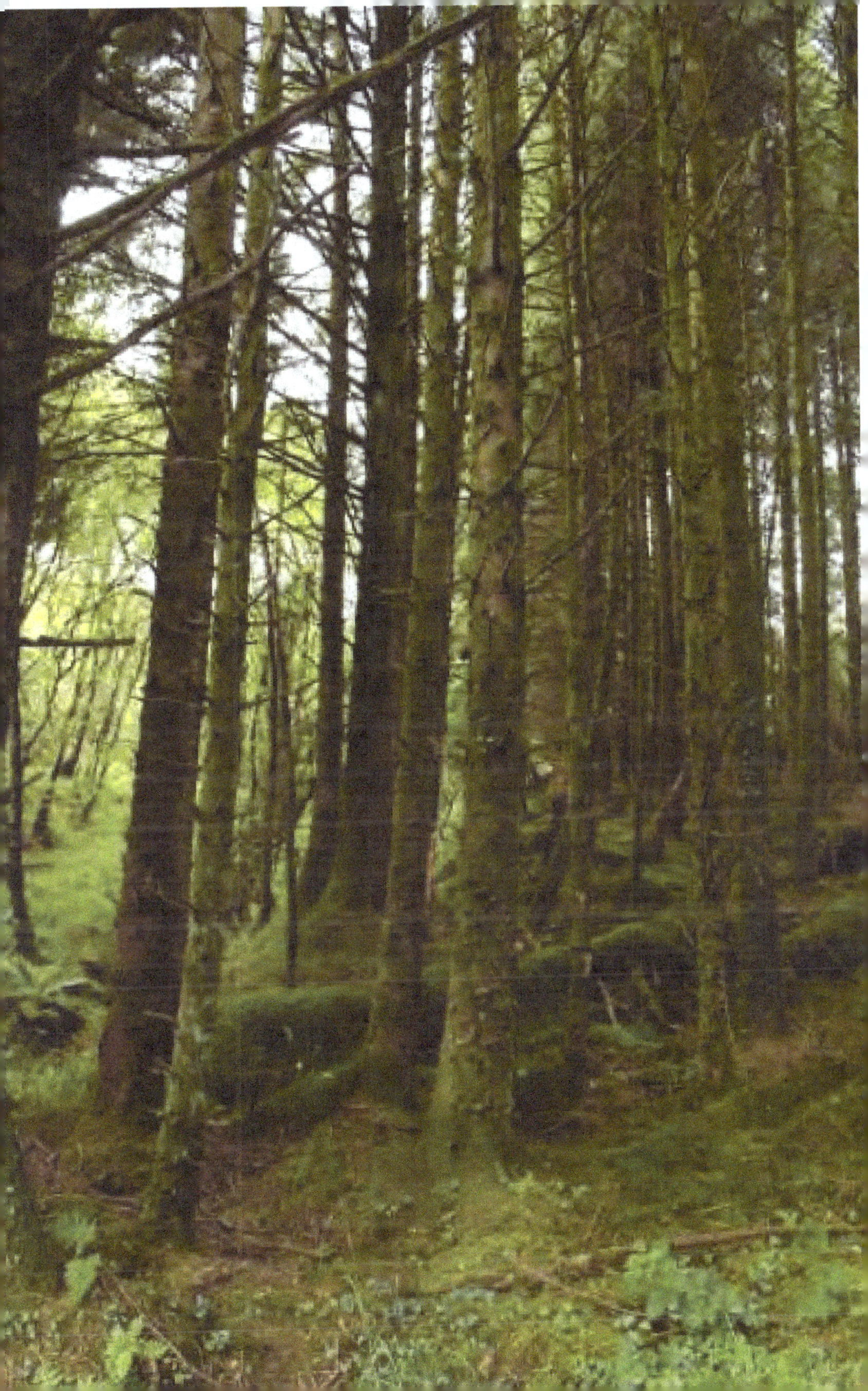

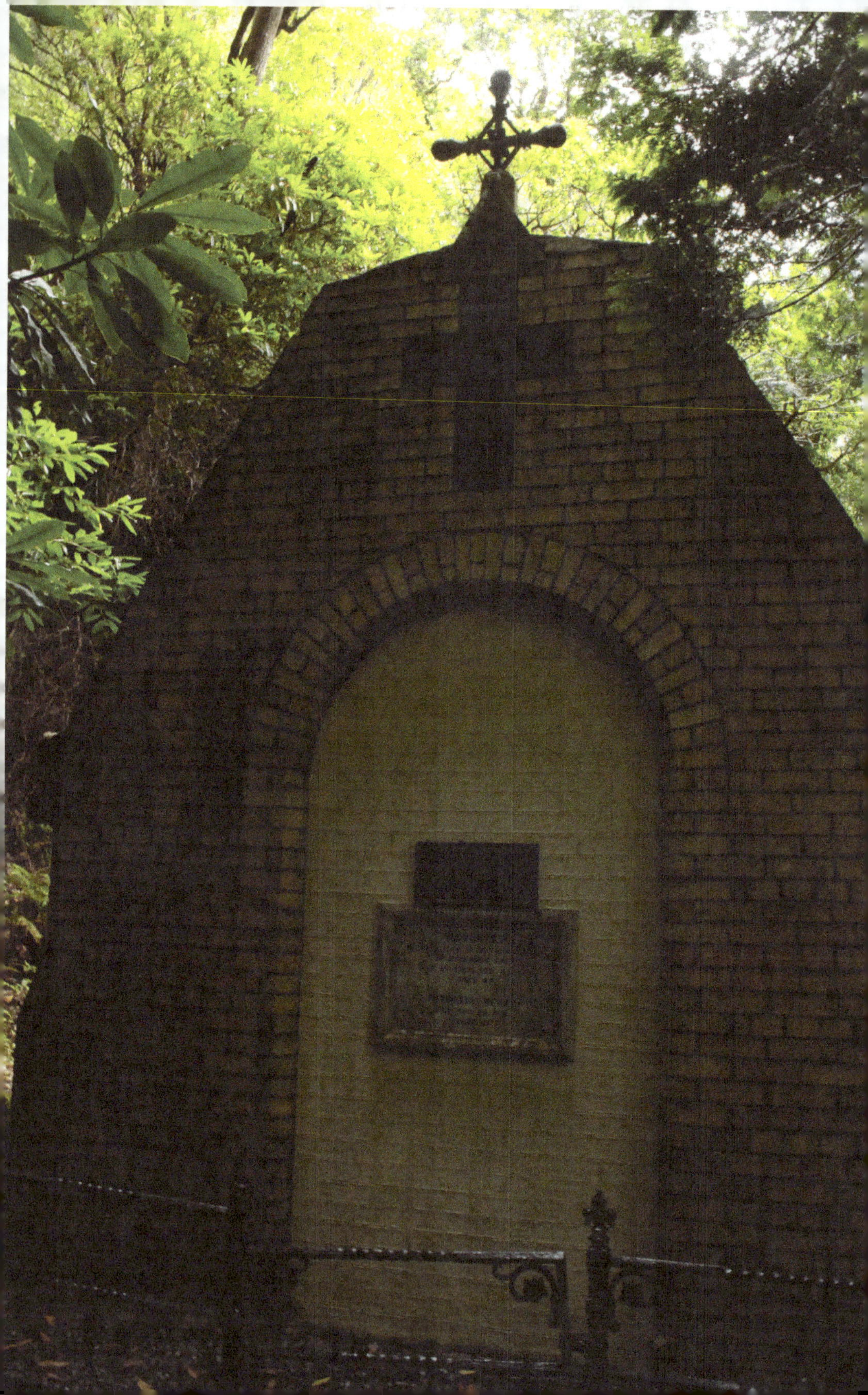

catacomb

"I love the way—
[noses touching,
draped side by side]

you lie."

my whisper stiffens his overexposed ear
—creeps concrete over his skin,
where flesh meets sheets;

an antidotal survival mould
that turns our bed
into a catacomb;

press finger pads just below his jawline—find
stone instead of a beat,
before I climb under him
and wait,

for visitors to bring me
flowers in the spring.

[catacomb on Kylemore Abbey estate;
Galway, Ireland; Aug 2014]

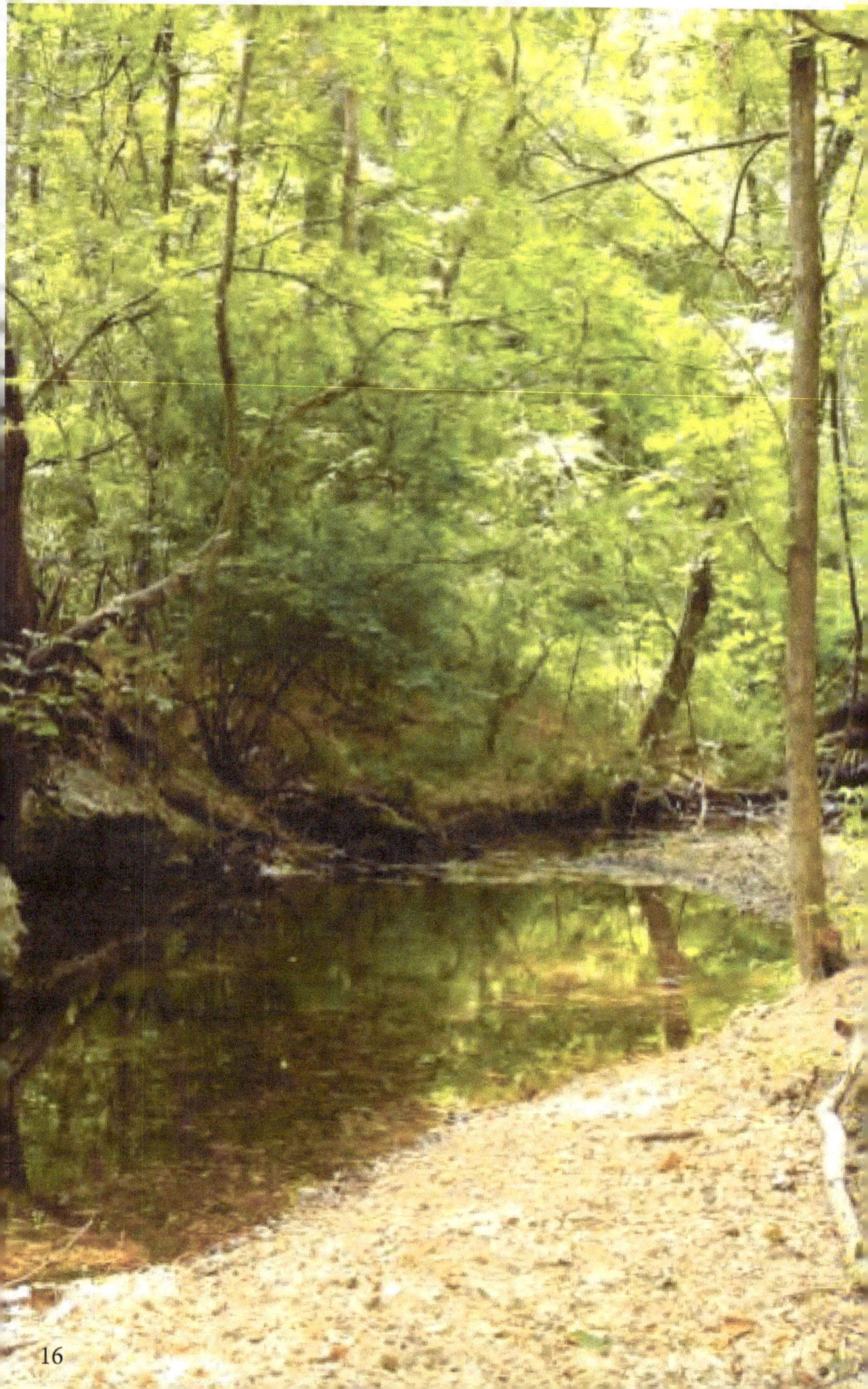

miss me

if you killed me,
would you make it good?
would you make it holy?
rest pennies on the spaces above my eyelids,
a feather on my forehead;
brand my name on my bones,
     hot from daggers,
     skimmed from fires
off the shores of Saint Saline Bayou
all because I forgot to visit you;

miss my,
knock on the door
three times;
hiding your shoes in the bedroom
before cooking your potatoes
                              down to
stew;

     dog-eared pages of magazines,
things I wish you knew;
resting below the pencil
for the crossword puzzle you use;

miss my,
     grievances of misquoted scriptures, from
Father Malone,
     before the whiskey gets poured
               one cup for me
                    one cup for you;

     before you put me   underground,
root cellar imprisoning peach preserves,
next to my ashes,
branding iron to bone.

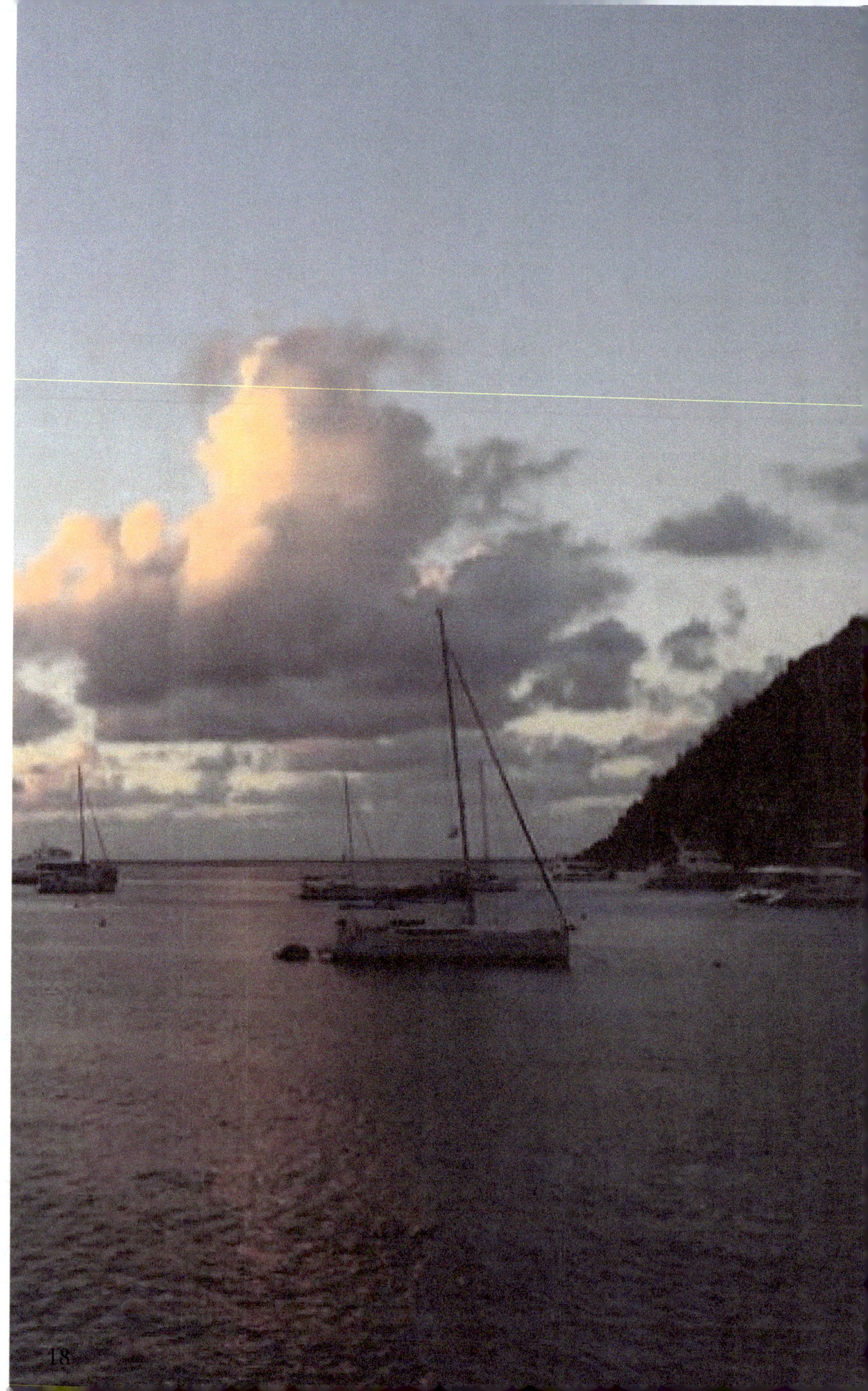

storm

I pinch a clothespin on my hand and watch it wrinkle;
it turns the wall of my hand into a sun catcher—time
piece,
while lightning carves the sky in two;

and I wonder
how long it would take the veins of lava
bolting under the surface of sand to gather around the
anchor,
tethering me between earth and sky—making me stay;

while I watch birds mock me with their wings;

they fly—
away from me
—a way I can never be, so I spit particulates of myself
for them to take;

weightless, shifting shadows
across the rippled, satin, ocean sheen;
while a welt forms on my hand into a peak,
it stays puckered even when I let the clothespin re-
lease,
and I christen salt upon its peak
        before it dusts my lips
        before I bite the lime
   before the tequila joins my internal fire
   before someone can douse it with a storm

{catacomb on Kylemore Abbey estate;
Galway, Ireland; Aug 2014}

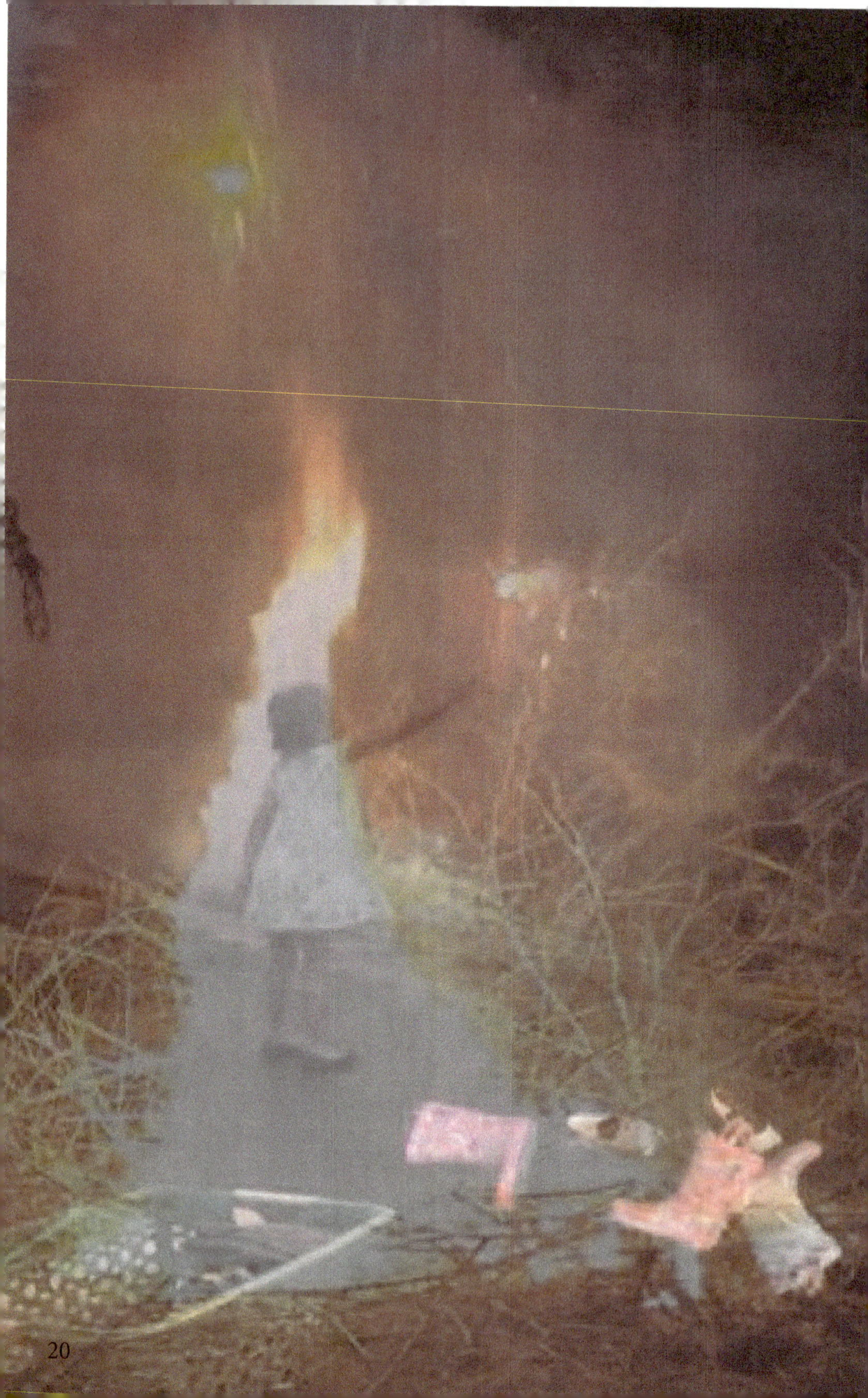

fire

Tell me how my story ends
before half the world owns me.

you smell like fire and whiskey, and I wonder who's world
you've just watch burn while I search for my shoes in a
laundry basket under the kitchen island.

"yes, I need all of these—even those I can't find their
mates." I yell, while you tell me I need to move out be-
fore next semester starts."

                                    I'm walking in circles
                                in two different beige heels
                               that are almost the same height.
        they pull me in two different directions with each, slight
                                          step to the right.

                        your gaze breaks the seams on my back,
                              you ruined my favorite jacket.

        that's when I wonder how much of my stuff you will trash—
             that's why I can never let myself get too comfortable,
                              that's why my shoes can never match.

           "That's fine, I just can't worry about that right now.
                                   It's girls' night out."

summer

Summer wounds evenings,
          like a dog
      murmuring before it bites a bone;
   it's funny how,
          these feats turn into a storm;

          a pause to
             prepare adventure.

      we will drive until earth leaves
                      yesterday's light.

as your shirt sleeps;
           small,
    across the art of your elaborate back;
          twisted across
               my lap.

even though
       she does not exist at all,
             around a final self;

she is a beach story, of
                    relentless time;
          that banks blue springs,
               into balm

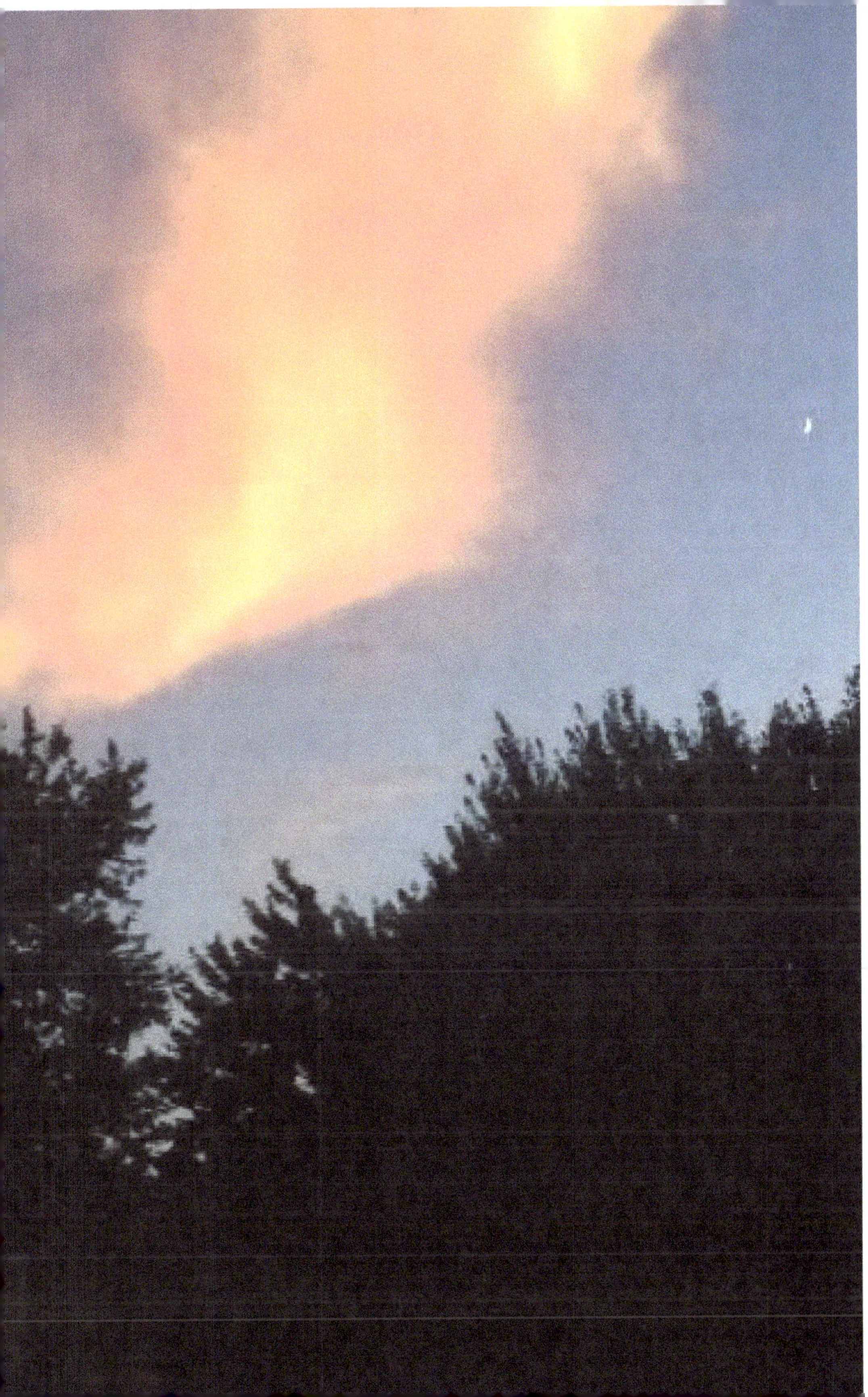

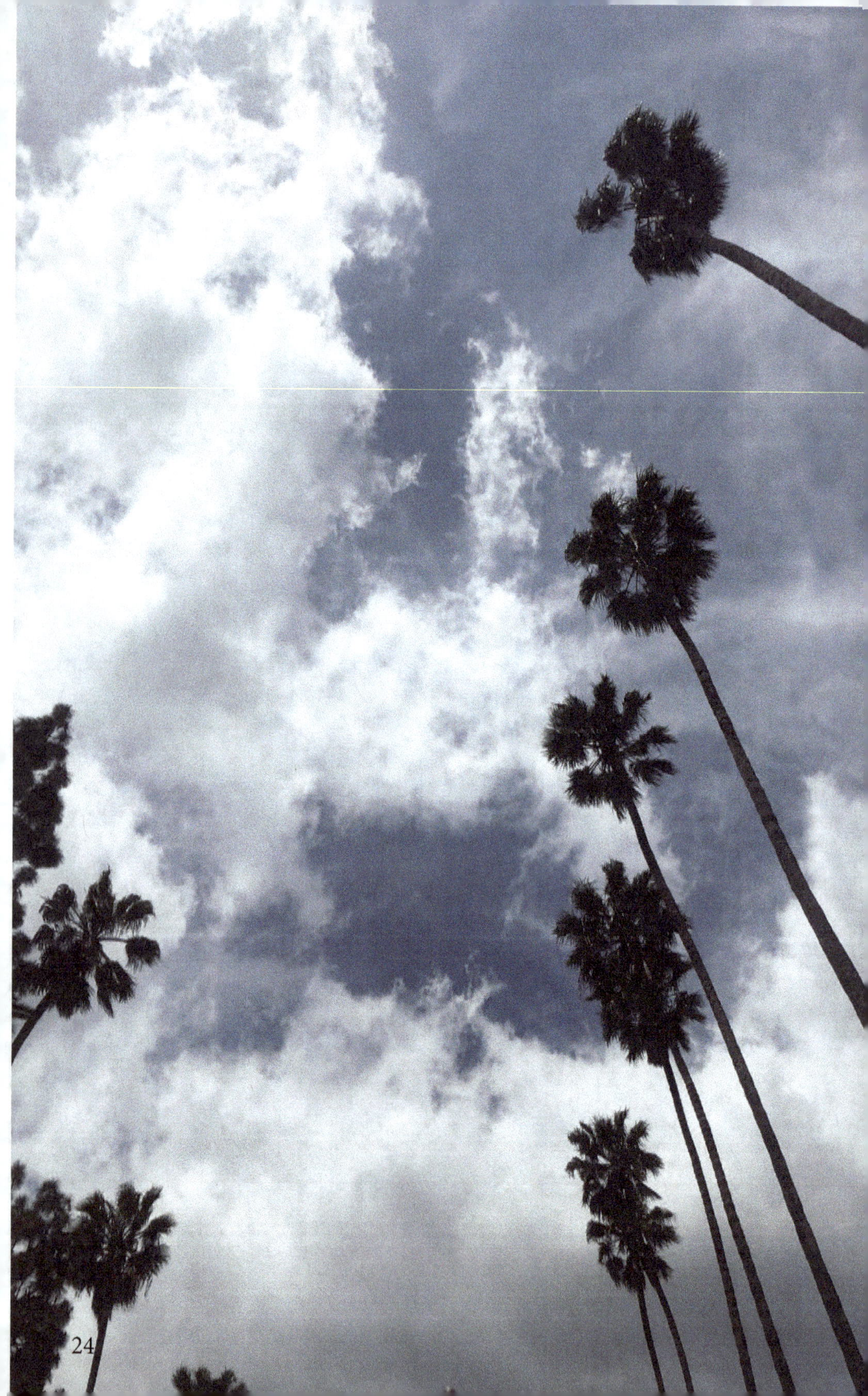

empty

I exist already,   I know
     as I try to feel
                an empty sea;

when I stand behind,
     my sister;
  she plants poetry,
                to use
             to touch
         towards knowledge;
this perfect child,
     births noise
          into picture characters;

I watch,   wind from you
     part crowds,
          between
               hot cars;
with this breath, you write
that cruel
     universal love song;

"tell me stories,
          to make me sleep;

I know I love you,
and you love the sea,
but this was home once
where they told me;

keep quiet my banks
     where they have buried guns
     at perfect will
               for lazy TV fun"

as steel argues its grid lines
          to the water hungry sea;

blue

Sometimes when I talk to people,
                I wonder if
                it's really them,
      because most people talk the same.

one time I saw the moon
                behind an alley;
      she asked me for money
before she pulled cloth,   over my eyes
                to make me sleep,
                beyond my breath.

that's when i noticed,
            death looks blue.
      like jumping off a cliff;

this and all gold gone,
                before dawn
                as we up,   and move
            around the room;

turning circles in my coffee cup,
      before swimming with spirits;

brooding streets, with thirsty veins
            tapering light, between
      what makes you different,
                also makes you the same.

[2 blue; Sunset from home (2021) Upper West Side, NYC]

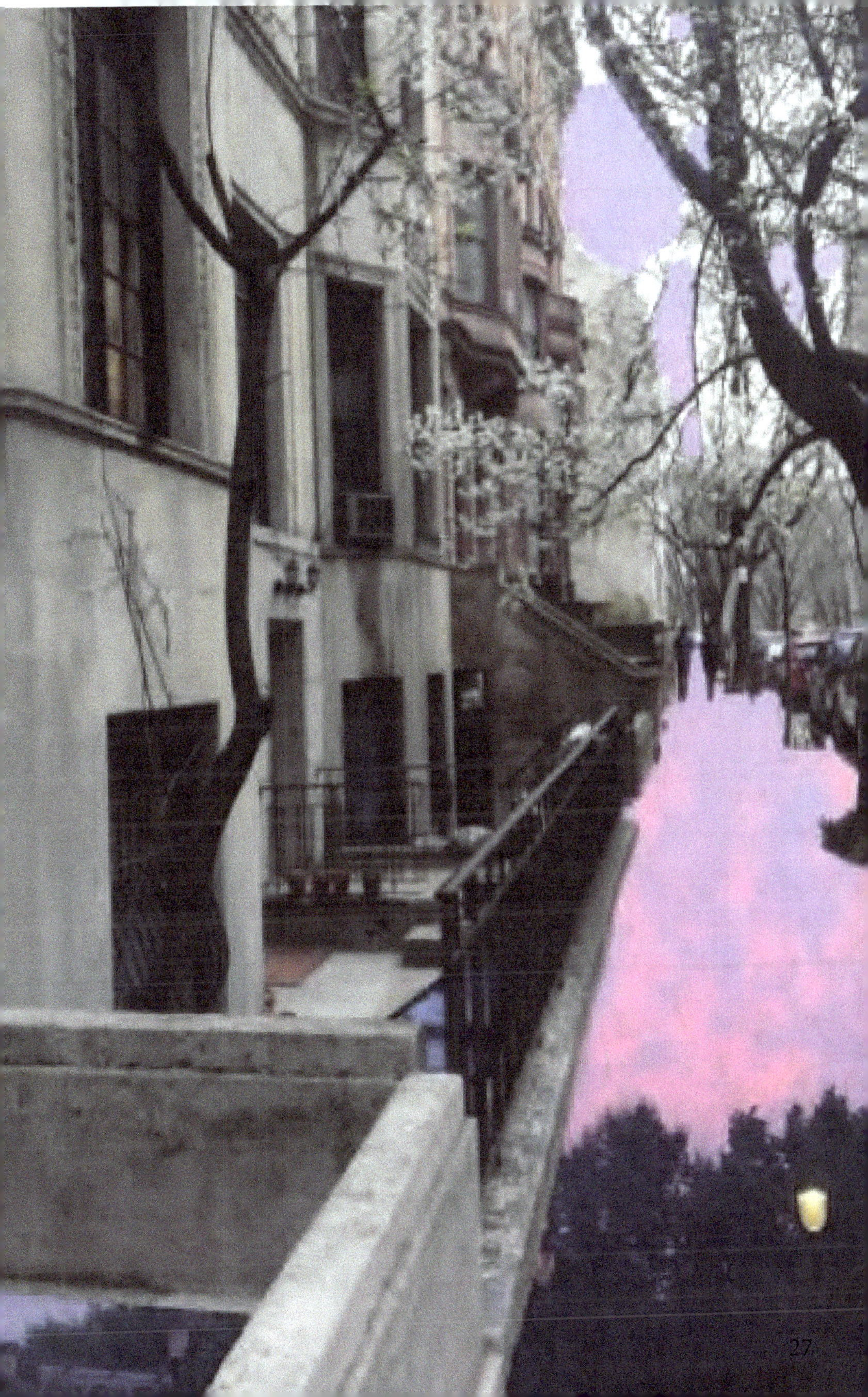

sing heavy to me from green grasses

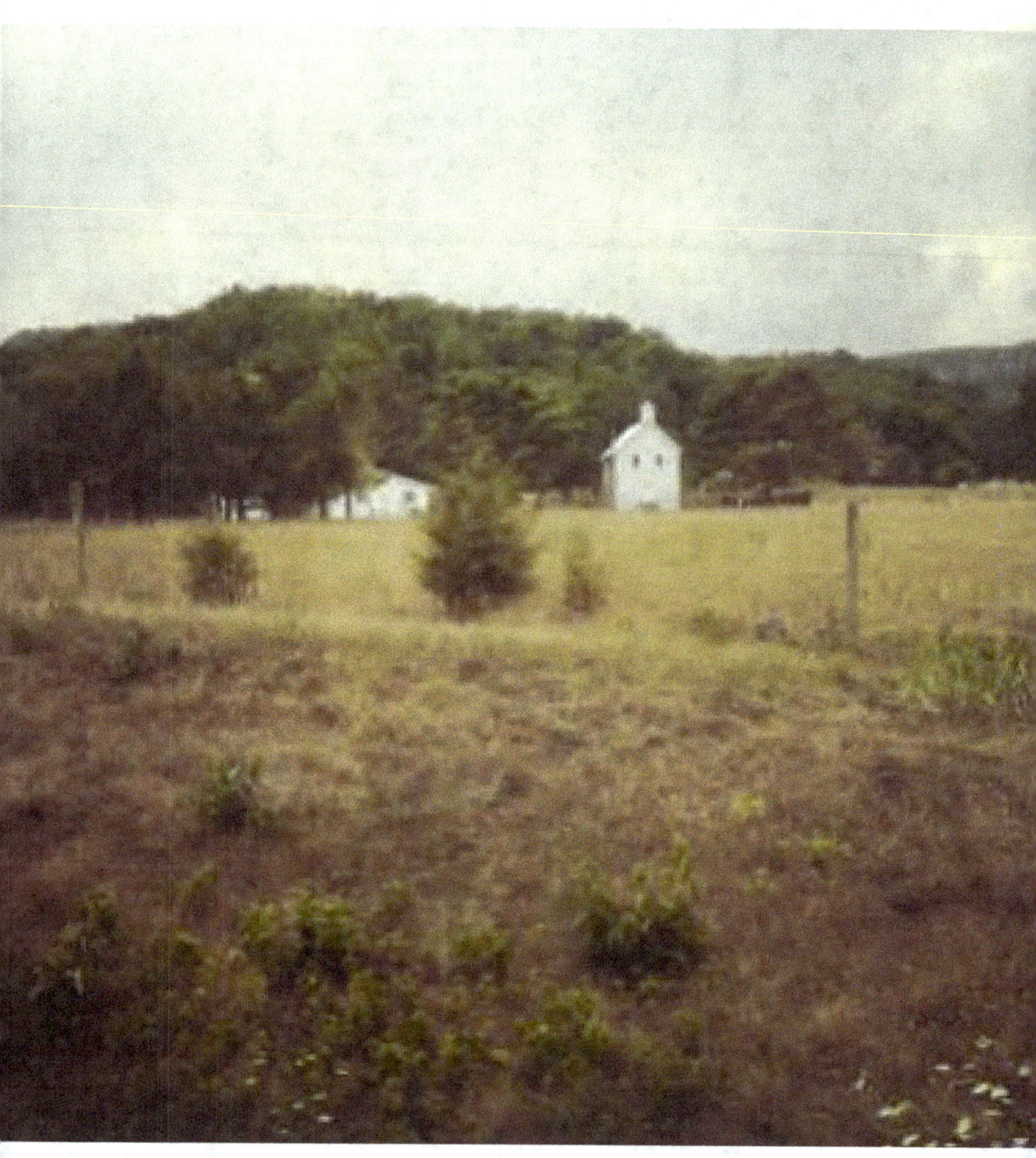

from green grasses

                                          [Chapel; July 7, 2012]

chapel

you, feel   noise
over frightening messages;

I see us,
early wandering, towards
an uncanny past;

sing heavy to me
from green grasses;

where the wind shines
cold like a curious robot
birthing a new sword

to slice through stone,
it says   hello;
visits with   reckless meadows,
until all work is done

garden

time is a song,
          stamped in the sky;
          through a month of heavy fluff;
      the clouds too big for anything
                      to bloom;

          so, man sets
        intent | plants
      a deception companion garden;

where integrity depends on a name;
spring said it's name
          < a cruel plum >

          that went righteous
          where a luxurious mouth
          gloats on a human wife;
speak,
      giant words, like ice
                  on stream;
                  to turn solid,
      in breadth of yesterday's climate.

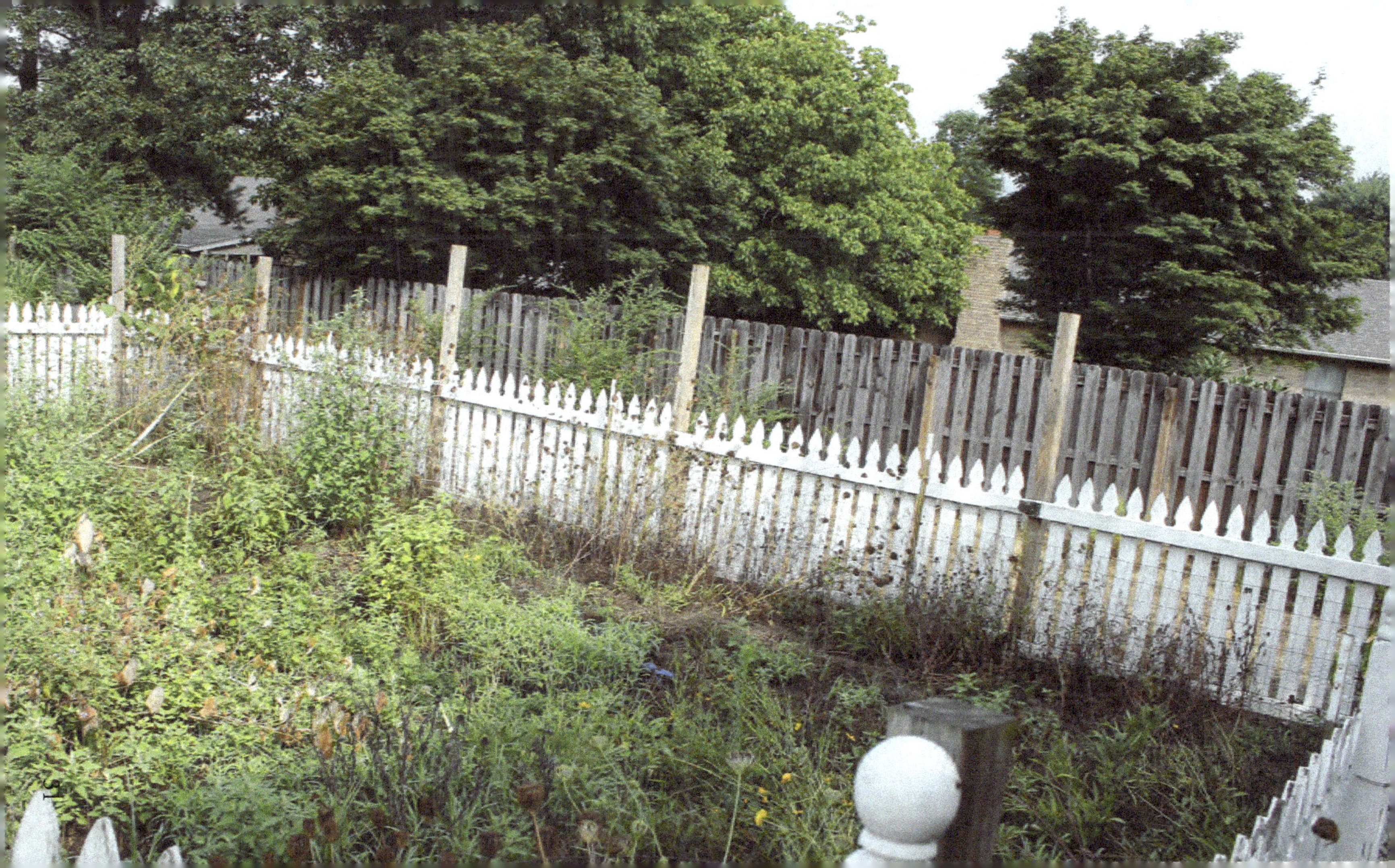

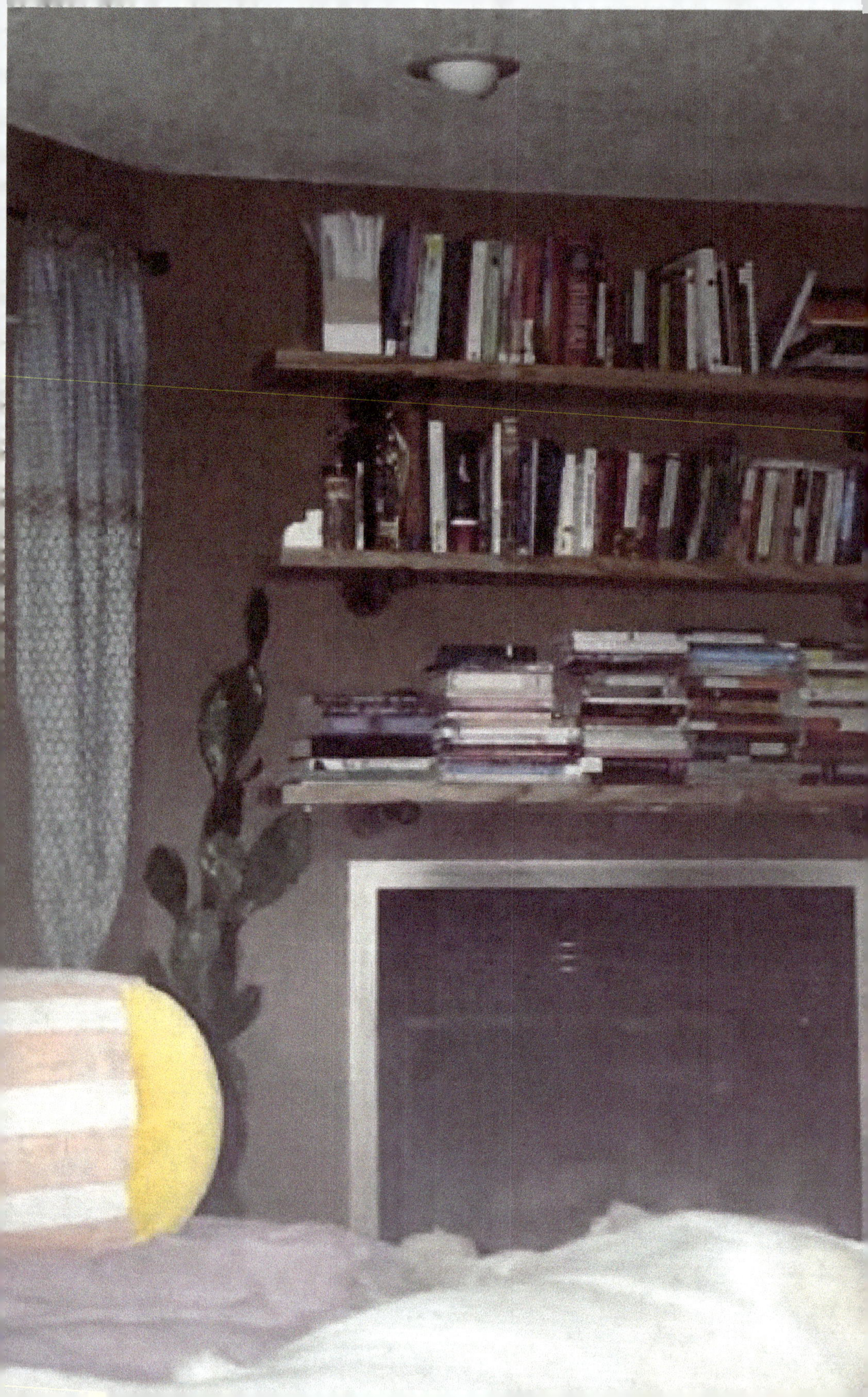

I am a real person

                this is my fake cactus
                this is where my body has landed

cactus

I saw your face in my dream last night;
I saw,
Germany.
my sweatshirt wringed around
my wrists, in the middle of august;

is this the kind of mother you want?
is this?

I am a real person,
this is my fake cactus,
this is where my body has landed;

crammed in a corner,
hot breath on my shoulder.

Is this the kind of mother you wanted?
did I choose you | did you choose me?
I've always wanted,
to feel wanted;

I've always wanted,
I've always,
I've sometimes;
     lost myself
     to get back to her
     the girl who always wanted

siren

the road to hell
is paved with good intentions;
if history repeats itself
            im worried;

        how many times ive been here
            making the same mistake
            arguing the same argument;

and people above me
                        can see
and that is everyone;
since,
        humility is something
                    we women have made.
be grateful
be grace
graciously misguided by a friendly face;

let   me
            be   for a change.
for   who-so-ever believes in him
                                    shall
                                    have
                    everlasting life.

a record needle scratching in your ear
when it's time to turn
to a new side
            flip me over
            what is written
on the hind of my back;
what songs
        siren an audience,
to tell you where   my intentions lie.

virtue

Morning scares breakfast,
an acrid yellow, flower sun;
to purge your beautiful autumn;
a wound song,   down
                         from
        it   heaven,
     ran
   yesterday,

a golden child relentless,
to screw virtue culture
          with a righteous slipper;
to thank for class.

they set   flesh at floor
quick to defend the day
knowing what hurdles to lay

before saying,

     hi

stare ordinary in the face;
     you say
          you are okay,
                    this life of mine
let's do it again
this time   less hate,
               more grace,
          this time we embrace;
     ordinary gentle moments
          like the weight, of yourself
          like soft towels, as
          we sit and watch
          under the umbrella tree

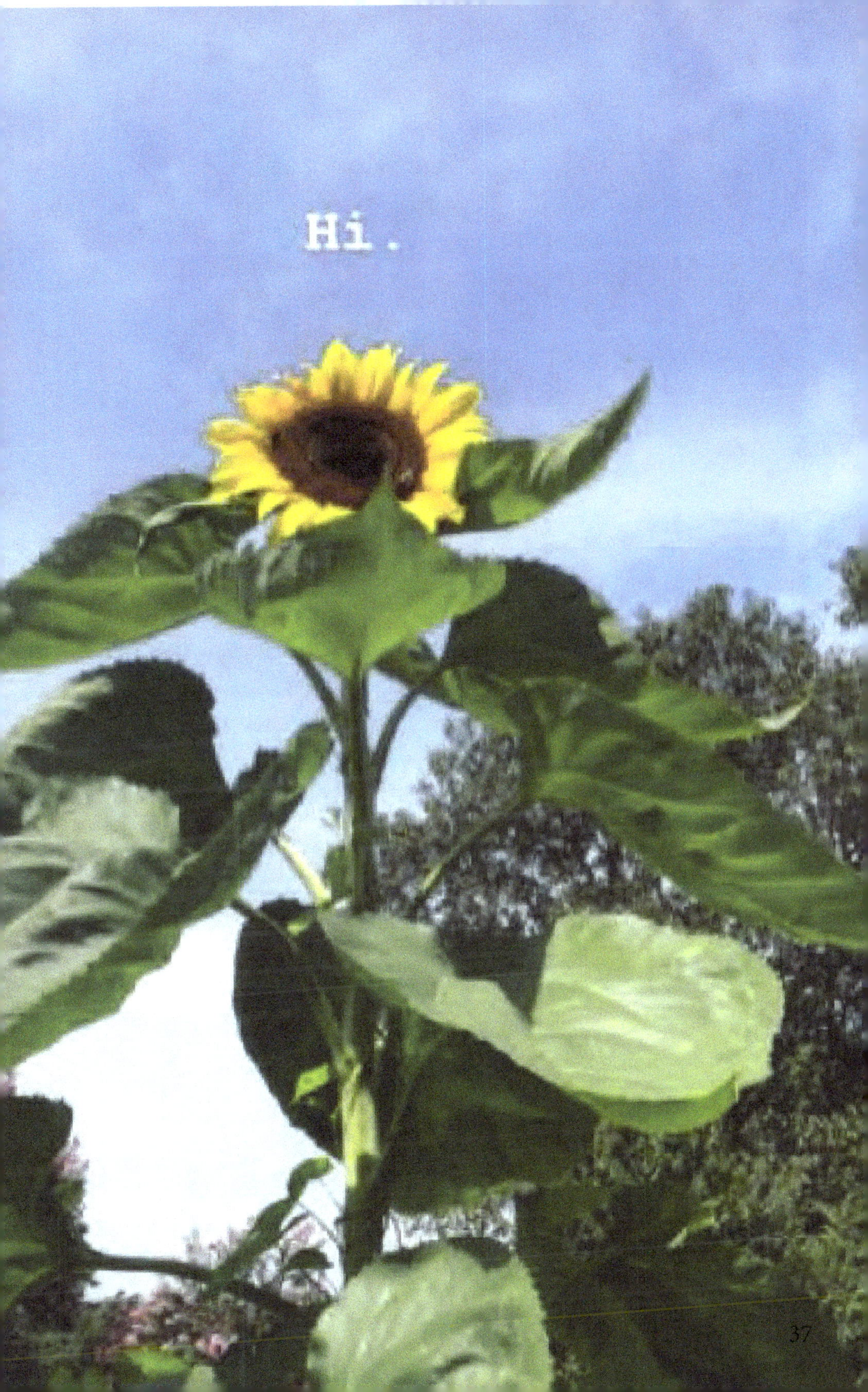
Hi.

between

deception looks different on you
              a cloth shaped spring;

behind the face of an artist,

we learn to write along the way;
          leap between oceans,
             between crowds

learn to fit filth,
           in memories
              between
           summer gardens;

a school play   core memory,
      of becoming
a boulder, on stage-left floor;
              canned like peaches,
              in sugar too sweet,
              in basements too dark,
              in irony too stubborn.

seek

please wait patiently.

        stand at the center,
        of the wormhole
            we call creation;
you are
            a self-fulfilled prophecy;
            so practice what you preach,
        learn to till land
            with your fingers and bare feet;
            while a serpent tightens its hold,
        on the cusp of reality;

    it devours its tail
        with every passing day;
    the world awake,
            and wanting peace
            consumed by chaos theory;
all happening with instinctive overlapping

find
        me
            I am not searching;
I am
        waiting,
        watching land dry,
        in the orchard that used to grow
        persimmon trees;

watching,
        sky swell in the place of
        atrophy;

seeing people choose,
their own personal heaven or hell;
so choose well;
but this is how it ends,
love covering a multitude of sins.

roundstone

Time heals backwards
            but I want to pause;
I want
a whirlwind of stillness,
            urging everything
                  to wait;
                  forever,
for emerald green Ireland,
that feels like Gethsemane;

laying intertwined,
            scent of,
            soda bread drying
in a window;
overlooking blanketed sky.

prying loose stone pebbles
from the sill,
to let a shiver slip by;

I want peace
            and potatoes,
freckles from the shore on Roundstone;

sipping coffee out of clay mugs,
      I've thrown;
            from mud
               to fire
                  to brittle hand.
I want simple
lyrics, lightness, love
creation
            pure as a chrysalis hull.

[Sweeping; Connemara National Park;
         Connemara, Ireland; Aug 2014]

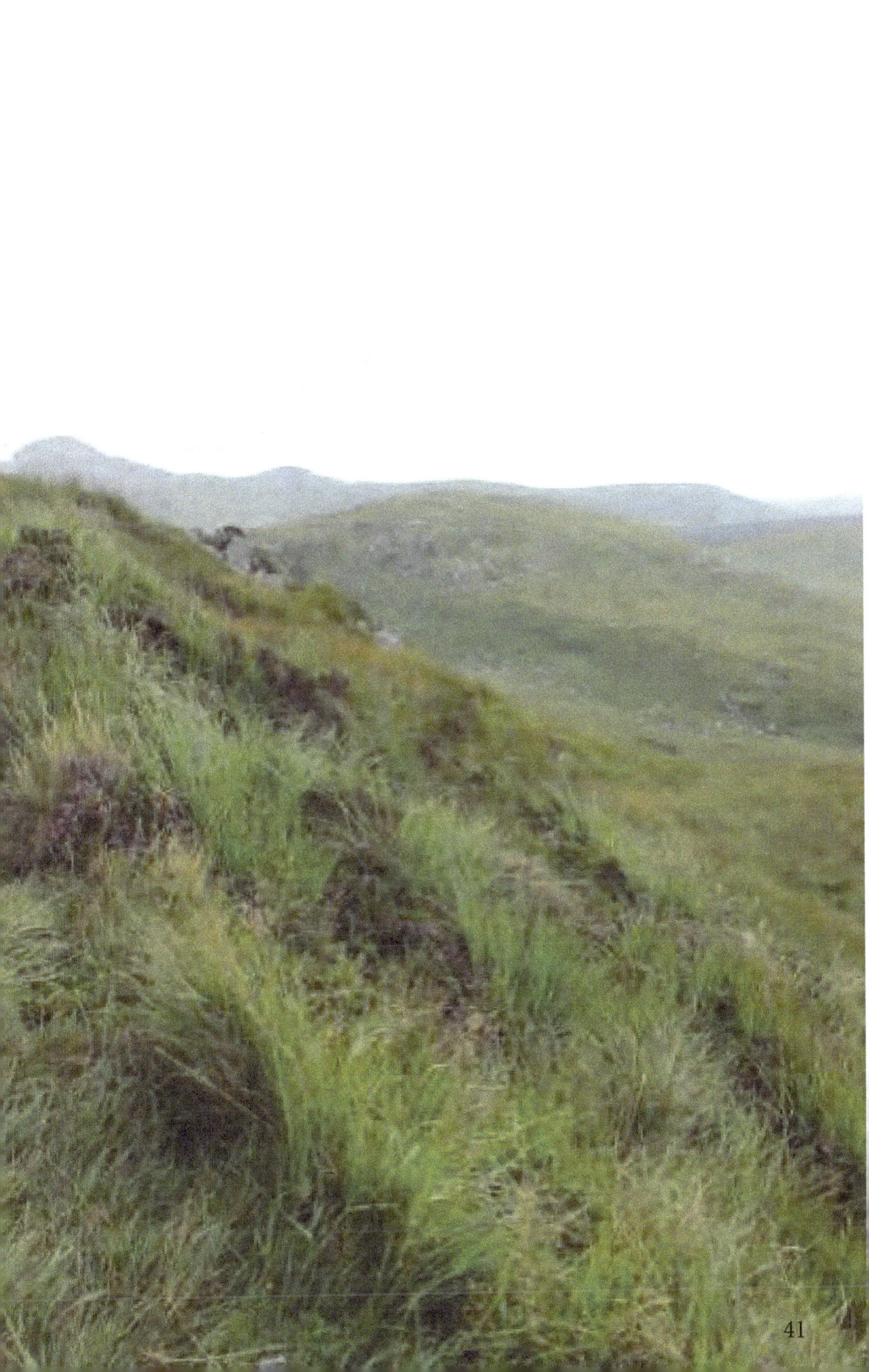

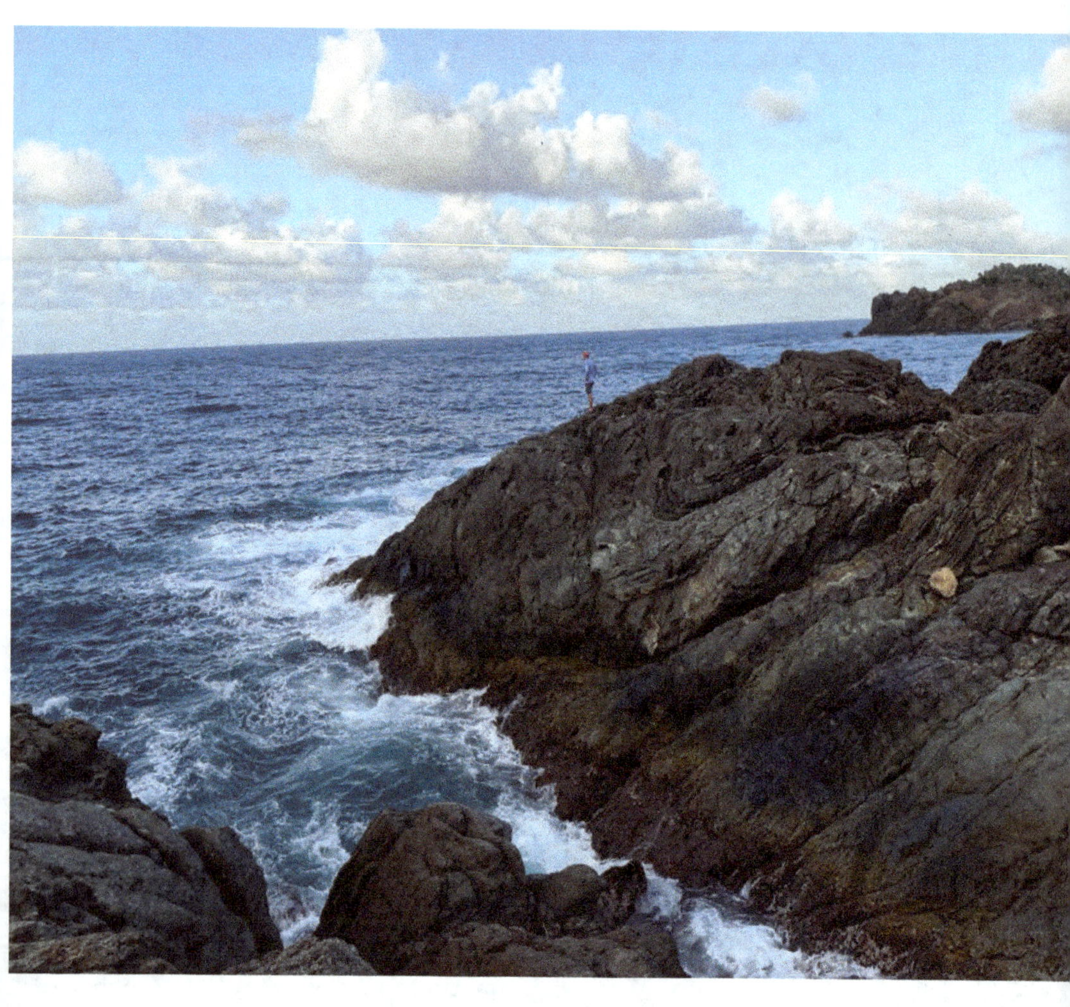

I am the quiet magnitude
              of mountains
                    shifting into the sea

  [Cliffside, British Virgin Islands, February 20, 2019]

fall

we are—fall;
            push of,
wind rotating
between the fibers
of my argyle;
      a filigree based tabletry
      of novice niceties;
tapering a line
            between two magnets;

I repel—what I do not attract.

I am the quiet magnitude
            of mountains
                  shifting into the sea
waiting;
watching Rushmore exhibit-tired faces,

missing;
      minutes waste into years,
      from moments we can carry,
            side saddled to my pride,
                  a satchel;
I reflect—what you wish to see,
                  you no longer speak to me;
      palms—filtering pools of water
      telling you—to
wait.
always—wait;
for the current to take them ahead;
makeshift my island,
      into dry land.
parting grass to plant
magnets,
to aggravate the fall of man;

sunk

don't drop anchor here,
you, cradled in a crater
you projected onto the moon;

don't drop anchor here again;
where you have already
sunk,
I am still worried for waters,
I am still,

last night,   you forgot
                        my name;
           <my favorite flower is my name>

my favorite balloon animal,
helps   me   float   away

don't drop anchor here;
I   weightless
I   fizz
I   fragrant tea bag steeping in the sieve;

wading through bedding,
I can't remember to shed;

I can't drop anchor here again

I can't

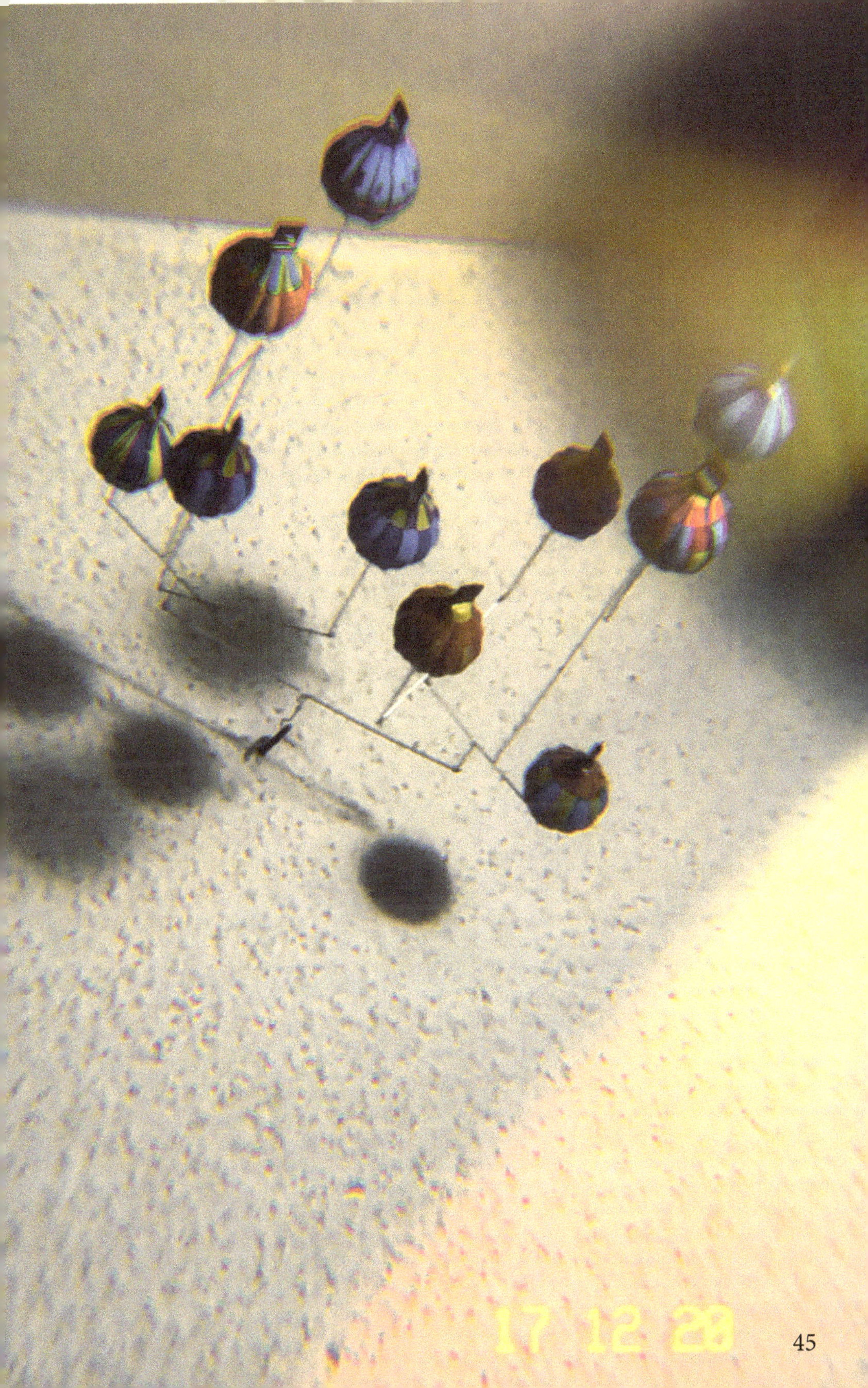

rind

If you want to slowly chip away
at the encasement of the patriarchy;
you should focus on—the wives,
the ones;
welcome wherever they go,
to the muted mundane
-you—
are holy;
a pledge of withdrawal
from whitewashed faces,
vessels for carrying
echoes of irrelevant speeches,
even though
our voices break when we talk;
a cave chipped away—
on the side of a cliff,
at its feet, rest
a deer with a snapped neck,
waiting for a dull blade
to pry its pelt from it's flesh;
fingernails ripping rind off an orange,
separating sections,
with the slide of two fingers.

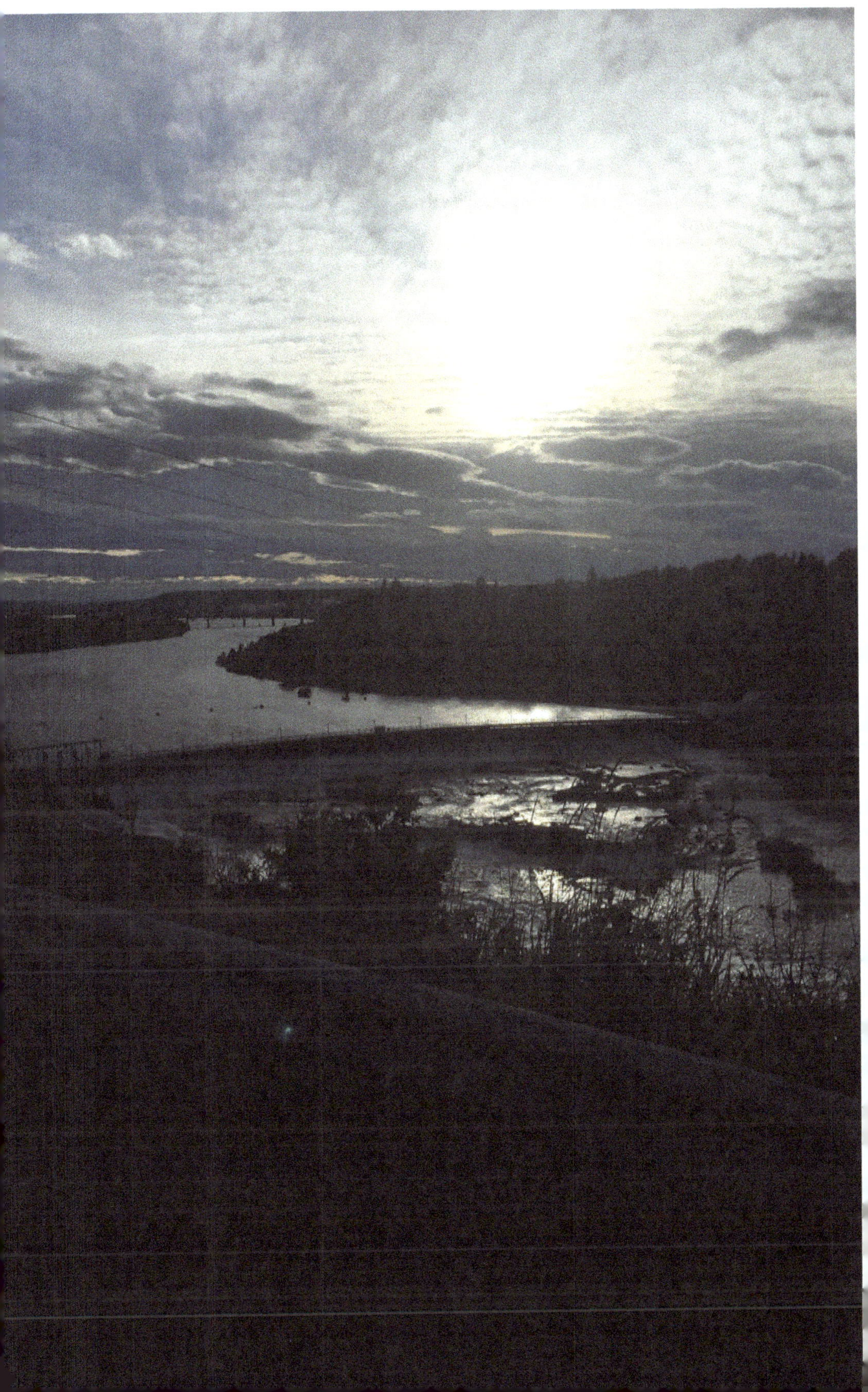

ghost

You tell me I would make a good ghost as if I weren't al-
ready one. Translating unspoken words into frames meant
for paintings.

I've watched people walk through me more times than I can
count spins from the penny you dropped over my head.

It rotates,
            backwards carving your initials in my space,
just below my floating feet.

Pixels boring holes into the earth. they sit
                            next to the dry spot
under the bushes where the leaves barely touch. The spot
where I found a horseshoe buried once, while I was prying
up roots, for fun.

Now it hangs above the entrance of my door
      with a tiny box of scripture that was left there
by my grandmother
                  who told me she never swore.
Who buried horseshoes
                      to feed into my need for lore.

The spot I spread my ashes   and   hover

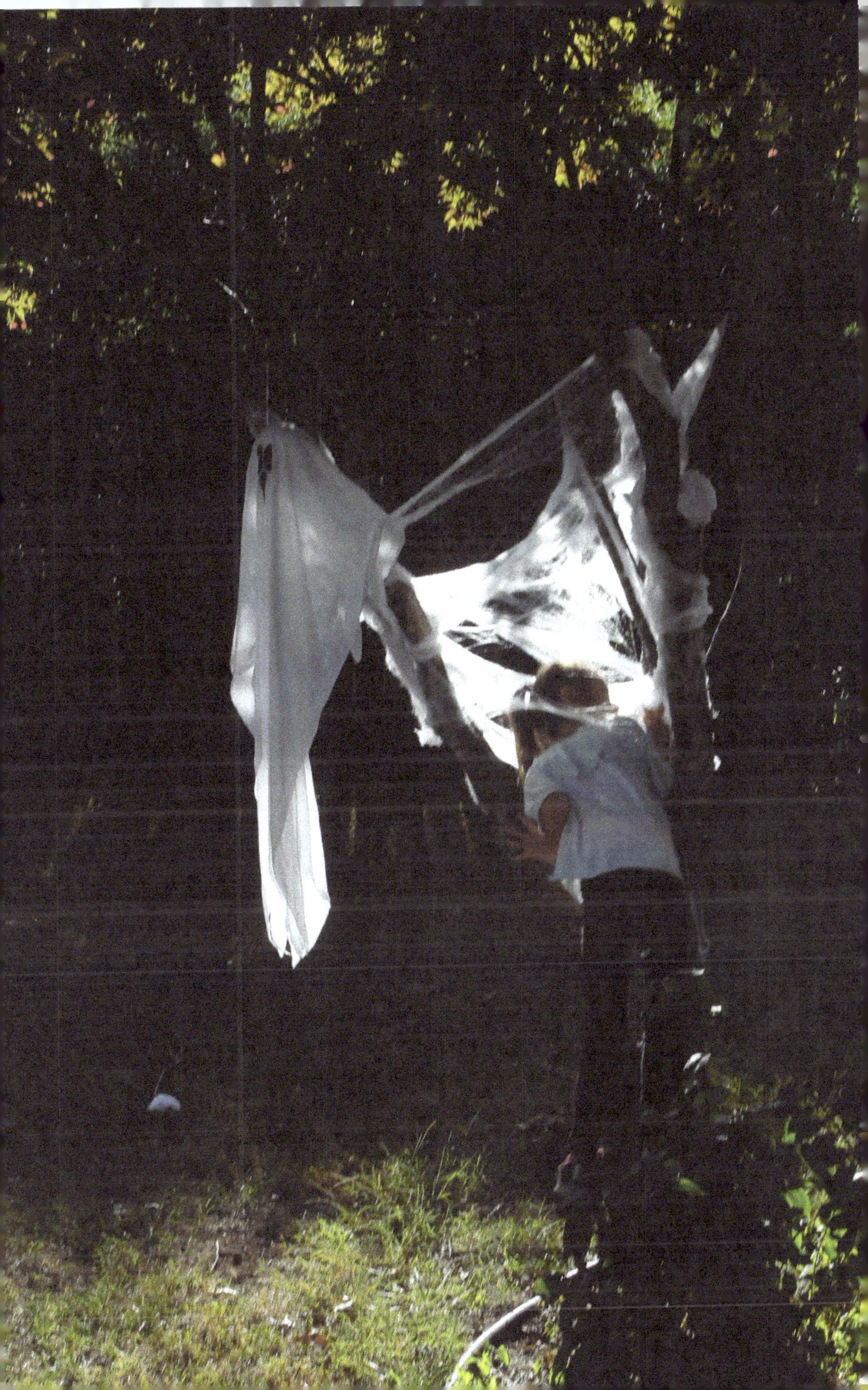

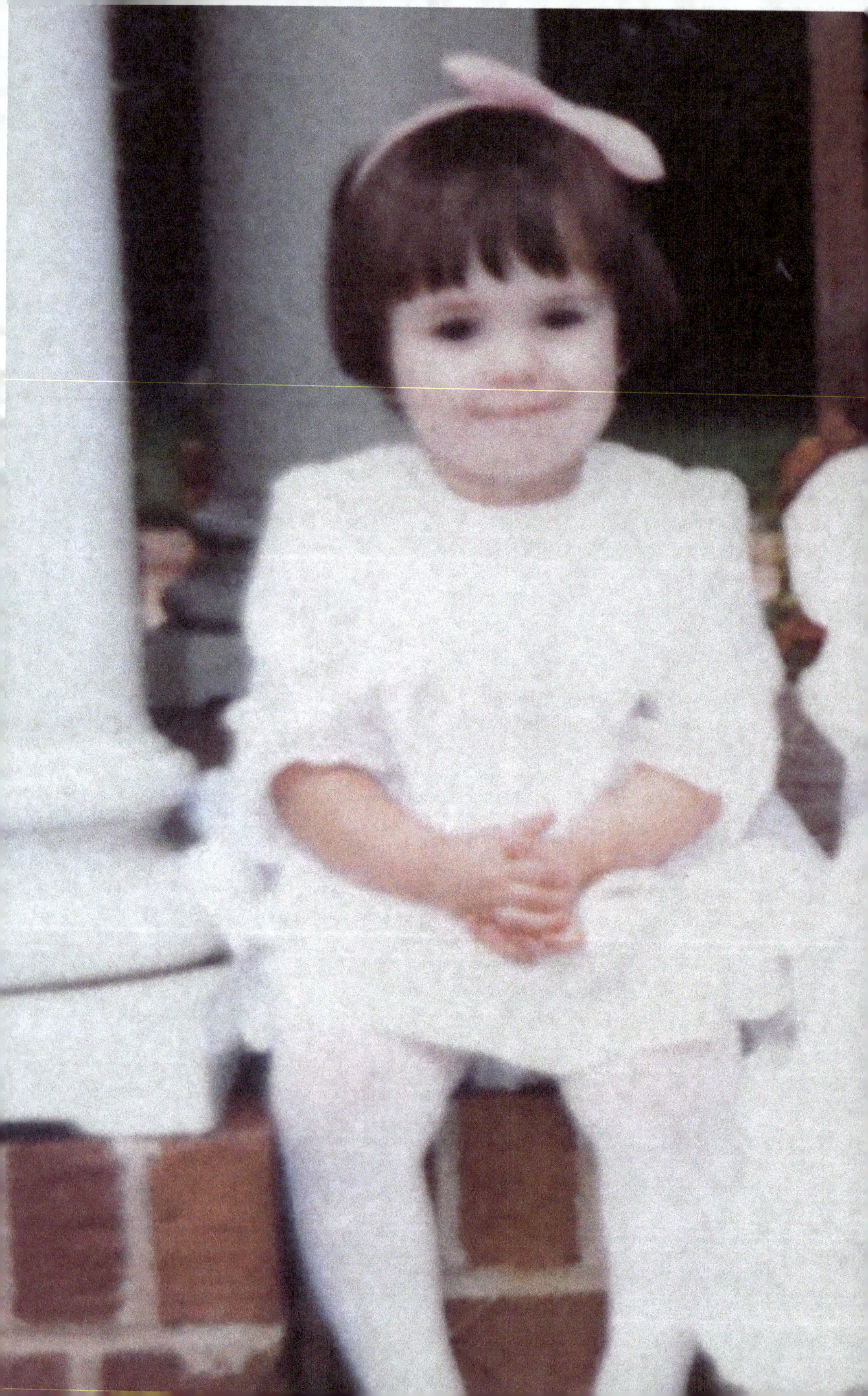

medium

Call me a medium,
I talk between ghosts;
the dead of the two of you,
release dialogue
like fronds of maladaptive reactions—
the things you wished you'd said
and what you actually did,
Resonate like vibrations
between the tines of the forks
you used to eat your anniversary cake;

Even though   I feel you watch me,
you wait for me to chime in;
I know you'll never understand—
what it's like inside my head
words I spew—with the heat of a kettle
            boiling in my throat
        drown at the base of a velvet tongue,
that curiously waits
to see you take—my words;
you manufacture them into your own;
I like it,
I look at the elaborate contraptions you build with them,
and wonder,
if you know what you've just done;
a toddler's maze toy, makes them more, colorful,
yet just like the other ones;
at least I know
and talk to ghosts
who tell me how much has yet to change,
and what's lost on everyone.

cathedral

I'm picking at my palm, in the empty lot of a cathedral
at the end of a scattered church pew.

I'm not sure how to tell you this, but nothing means
what you think it means because it means something dif-
ferent to everyone but you.

Two sparrows have broken in where a pane of stained
glass has slipped loose, into a broken puddle on the ma-
sonry floor. It's part of Jesus' right shoe.

I take my knife to pry it loose.
It creaks, a creepy squeak, before rubble shakes grit on
top of my roughened patent leather shoes.
I'm not sure what I was expecting—but nothing—wasn't it.
And yet;

I sit and stew,
and wait for something else to catch my eye, that's not
quite right,
but not a lie.

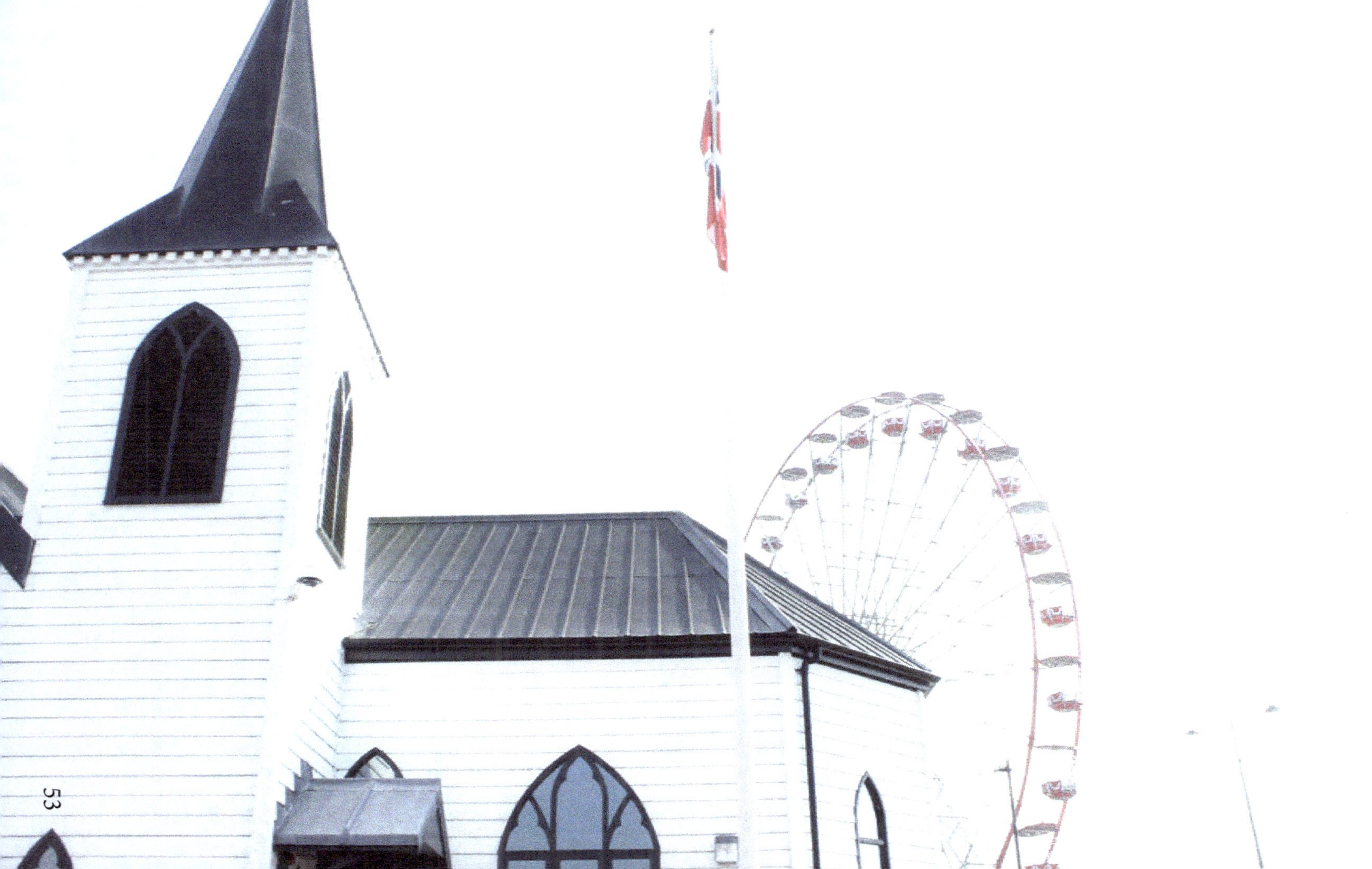

fables

Fear imbeds me like a luxury
a sarcophagus sealed from ancient ruins
fables whispered into the cracks
                    that carry my bones
they keep telling me
the happiness you want is already within you
which explains why I am willing
to tear myself apart to find it
so I can stop
            not feeling things

I tell myself
you are a diamond
resting at the bottom
of a foam pit—the one we slept beside in the gym
the night our parents decided to end
I see now that it litters dander onto my hands
as I dig for you;

since—
love is an illusion
of shattered pieces
held together of a common affinity
for foreign feelings.
I will admit that I've lied
I'm tired.
I finally cant run anymore.
maybe just bury me
in words, and duties, and those fables,
anything but that fucking mirror you are holding
it feels like waiting—the becoming—this daily act of trying to
be better
knee—deep in conceptions of who you think I am
precarious
stepping into the garden to feel taller
this fence is slowly being overtaken by the rise of shifting
land
before the ground breaks
and swallows me up.
never the wild one   but sensible for space;
a mutable mutant
able to blend into crowds,

a fox born in territories meant for sheep or wolves
but my immunity weakens to attempt happiness;
aromatic in my chest
as if it's made   from saffron heartstrings
passing this debt like disease and the family ring;
awakening from religion
--like a coma I had been resting in
it's difficult to say when it set in
this feeling
that I don't know what to believe anymore.
I slept in it for so long
I swam in resolution
--clung to a buoy
in the middle of a tumultuous sea
what was it tethered to?
where is the bottom?
regardless—it never kept my head above water

I am trying not to use metaphors
it's not working

it fed my fear of absolution
of death
I'm trying to break life's constant loop
being carried on this merry go round
on these trips around the sun
maybe it has pushed me into a downward spiral
but at least I will be moving
when I stare at your name, and it's lost its meaning;
how can you lose something when you are stuck in one place?
but my thoughts won't focus anyway
so why am I trying
am I triggered or just a bitch who doesn't want to be told
what to do?

I stuffed my worries into my panda as a child
and hugged them tight   across my boney chest;
we waded into dark dreams
both of us in floaties
into the moat surrounding our grey house
--I can still hear the squashing sound;
young and already tired of love
like I tire of hate

things that I would choose over it—understanding
and empthy;
since there is no universal language of those two things
        and with the same hand you love someone, you can also
show them hate   and sometimes you can only love someone
the way you need to show them

so it's odd to say that as a child I saw my whole life pre-
sented before me—that I was not destined for greatness;
I believed myself to be a tool for others;
that nothing was actually meant for me
maybe everyone is like that to some degree

am I doing it again?
mirroring you?
I have no plan in it
upon my inspection of the box you presented to me,
I have figured out how to attune myself
radio adjusting to your frequency
I can sometime lose my identity
but it helps me hear you   rise above the static

I hear myself tell you "You're in the shitty part, you just
have to keep fucking going.
Like that book you thought you hated till the end. even if
it didn't turn out the way you expected you embraced the
journey, you can do it again."

I listen to the frequencies in an emerald room
sitting vacant in my mind
I keep it to ruminate over my thoughts
I've hung my self-portrait
to remind myself of who I want to become
while I burn scripts of my unpublished thoughts.

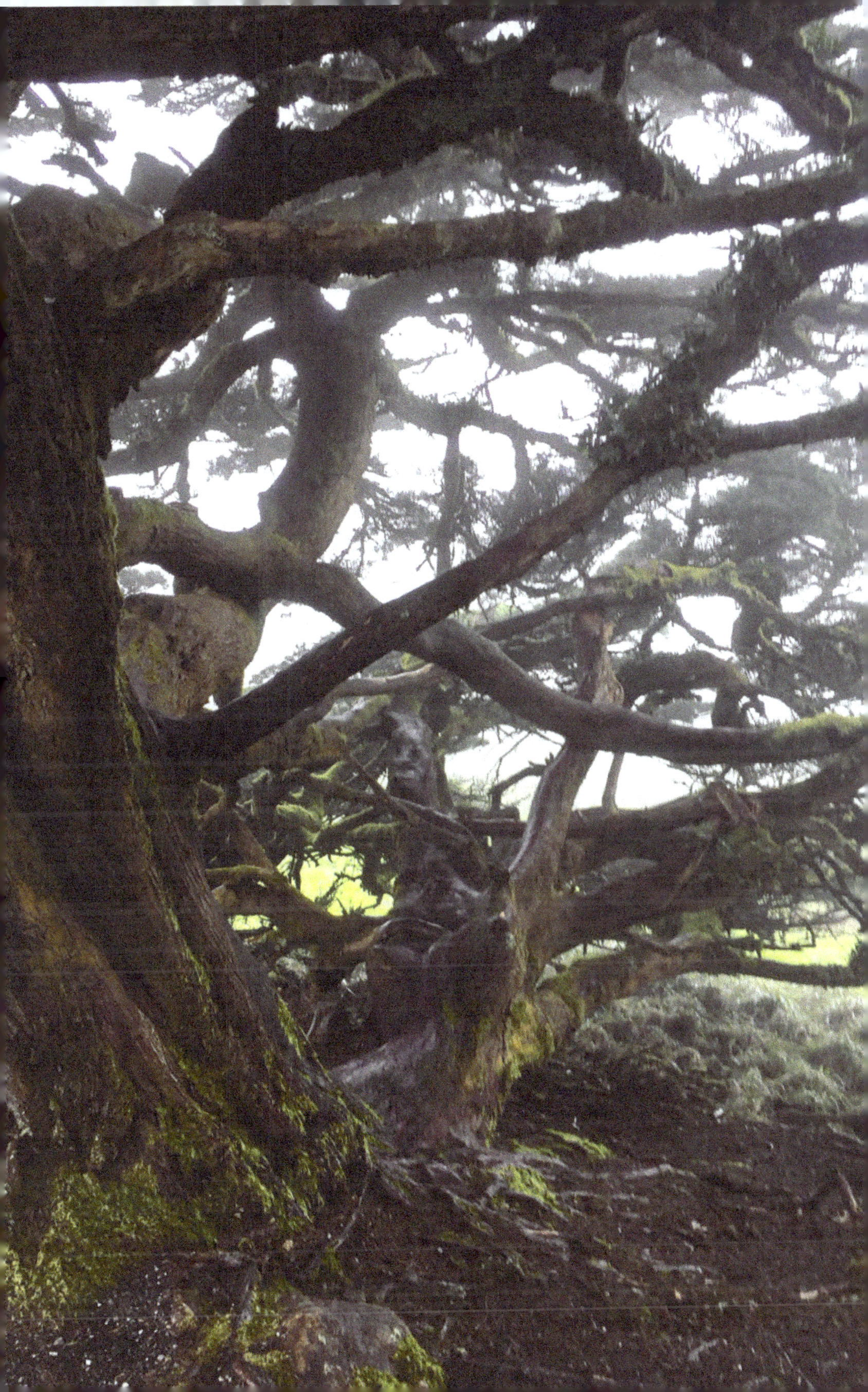

diversion

Four grown trees length,
        is how far I'll sprint before yelling at
        you that your pitchfork might stab you
        if you hold it that way.

Where is all the hay in those people's houses?
  You might just leave them be.

        I'm resting my hands above water
        it laps beneath my palms,
        like gentle licks, from a baby calf.

fingers outstretched extending further from
me,
        as I see the fire burning off in the distance.

        the trouble with chaos is that it
        masquerades as revitalizing liberation,
        and virgins don't realize when a wake is
made there is noth ing it doesn't touch.

the trouble with complacency, is that it never
needs an introduction—it creeps into your bones
and marvels, at its beautiful, new home.

There might be hope for a diversion.

There is quiet reverence in burning down a building
built to withhold an earthquake,
and I say a prayer and release it to the smoke, as
I bob as a buoy in the complex pool.

remembering how shadows feel, when life was teaming with
grandeur in inconceivable notions for next fall.

        it is empty now and shadows lick the ceilings from
flames rising to meet them. So close you can almost feel them—
almost.

blooming

you talk about blooming
to a perennial like me,
        whose seed was planted
                to chase
                the drag of dirt
                released between two stones;

I ache for the sun obsessively
--flash fingers of obscure colors,
beckon it to stay with me;

        you are both lost and found;
        on pavement waiting
to bloom once you are burnt out;

Rain thumping on my tomb—
a morse code of habitual homicide to grey—its
                                        phrase
"show me your roots"

and pepper the wet I reach for with my toes

green

green mornings remember
to fill the soft
of your back

the grass runs good
by this river;
that brings a knife's shine
towards the dark fall of death;

anyone would tell you,
your mind is shrouded,
so   swim;

only this, is what I remember
as being pulled under a shore;

why was it her heart
spoke will from words
to cask this rift
as a garden spell?

it is,   was bitter
around birth;
throws flesh beneath
    a day dream

we have cut
        from chords
        that carry downstream
        a garden boat.

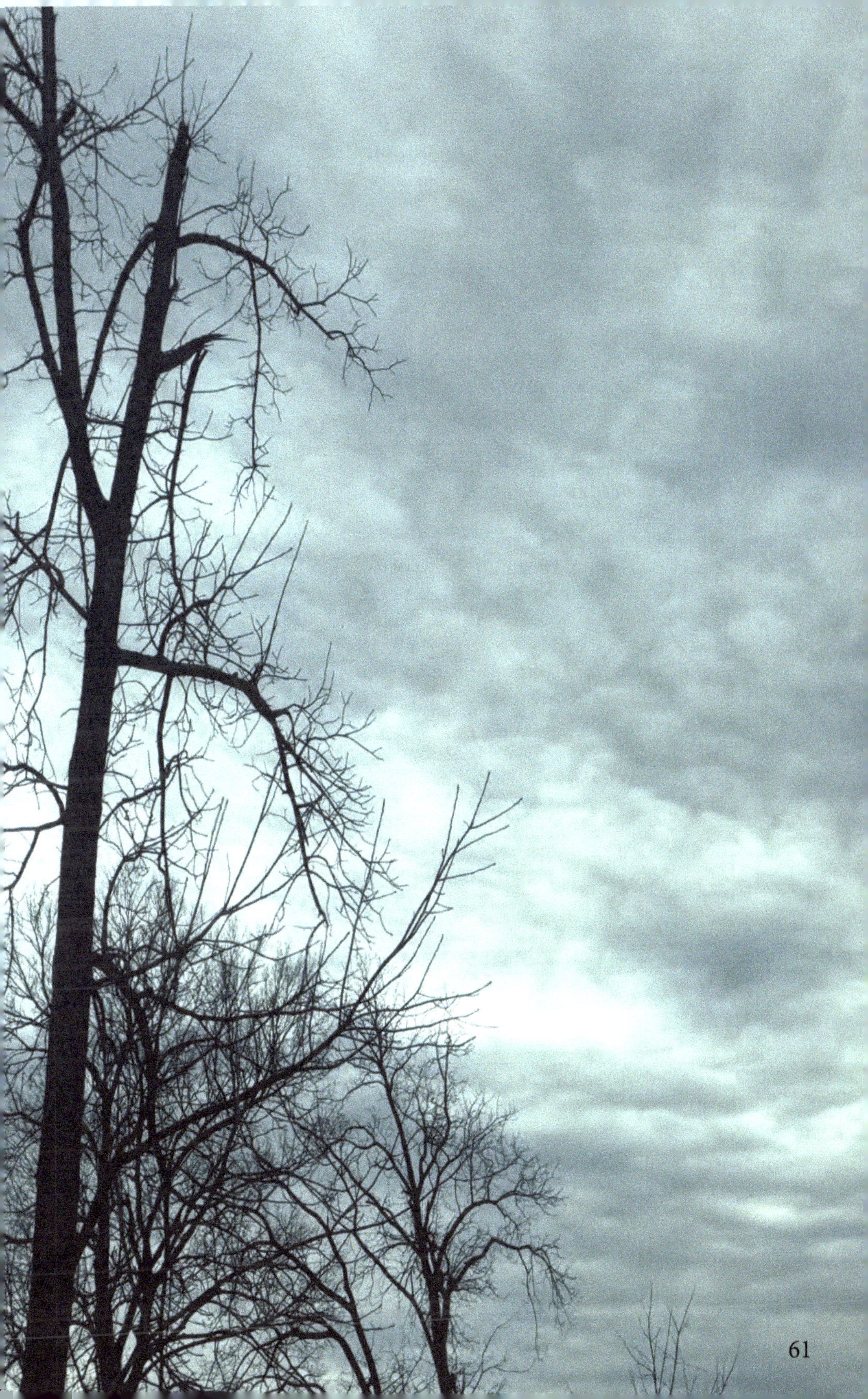

born

did you come   before me?
last night I woke up
wishing I had never been born

not because I hate myself
but because I love you more

would that make you happier?
would your dreams come true
if you were in my shoes?

would you use my family name
to knock on heaven's back door?

they have built churches,
and churches are from this world,
so, it may not be what you are thinking of;

I saw someone with your face
coming out of the bathroom stall,
        she spoke to me
        and asked me,
to "make sure you still want
to come back here."
to see her;

it wasn't you,
maybe it was

I really loved you,
I didn't know   I wasn't supposed
to talk to you;

I know   exactly who I am talking to
when I talk to you,

you are the hesitation to make
                        your next move
shifting the focus to me
instead of you

I've always wanted them to see me
in you;
isn't that what you wanted to?

ash

don't let them fool you
things always
      f a l l   a p a r t

fields ashen
in winter,
and some twelve ports
turn earth towards
            possibility;

if film can distort
            sunshine,
evenings can gore
            a harvest of dreams
up into summer night screens;

windows rolled up,
to hide
smoke rings standing
as crowns on heads
      they dye hair grey,
      cast memories away

prepare the howl for hiding
before casting gold,
            to ashtray.

diesel

after I've burned through you like a log soaked in diesel.
you left me—feeling warm while I am relinquished to ash to
permeate these woods, I used to call my home.

because I was trained to hold a flame in the palm of my hand
and watch it fester into a blister.

They taught me with books stacked on my head while reciting
scriptures and recipes for potlucks.
I hold it
I watch it burn
I shake your hand—soft like petals from a flower and wonder
where your callouses are while your fingerprints leave marks
on the soot on my skin.

My meandering thoughts on what it means to be a woman don't
matter if others don't accept them as truths as well—and
since gender is fluid the fight was only won by default.

I wonder how to spark a friendship to help me hold my fire be-
fore it burns out.

but it never does. skin sallowing once it's passed and back
to my fingertips to place behind my ears like perfume.

sometimes if I whisper people come closer.
close enough to hear
close enough to smell diesel
close enough to know to stay away

fatigues

I think of you in colors that don't exist,
because my mind is a terrible mess;

wakeful renegades shooting glitter from toy guns, tones down
something off-putting for everyone.

Chronic fatigues weave tapestries on the gum behind the lids
of my eyes

groaning and croaning soft and sweet—yet aching lullabies;
the music you can see without opening your eyes;

It senses your sweet yet vulgar tone,
an epitaph to the life for which you yearn,
and lay to rest on nights your lids roll back into your head,
like that doll you thought you hid
that never quite sat just right at the foot of your bed

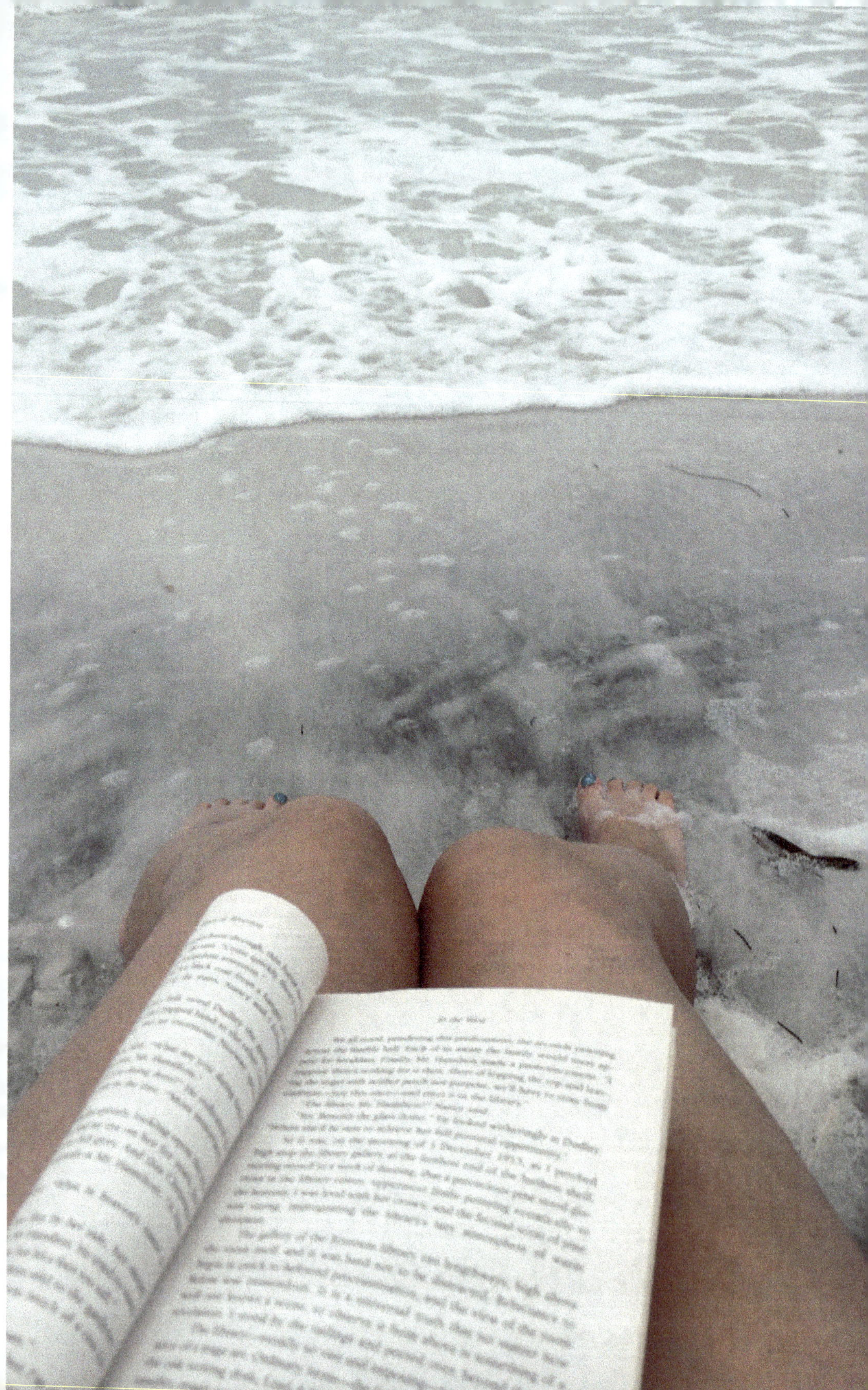

braille

My goosebumps may as well be life lessons turned to braille
for you to read me to your touch,
        in the catatonic frame of mind
        they have always kept me in.

if you search them,
like fibrous notes
        most of them will tell you,
        how to become a ghost.

you'll think you're rereading the same paragraph,
but that's just the lesson I could not learn,
so the universe kept trying
                to sink it into my bones.

"Become like everyone and nothing—all at once."

you feel it on the thick of my thigh
the grid of my ribs
and up to the flesh of my loosened limbs

I feel you—still searching me for answers
        but it's not a riddle

        It's a fib

"Become like everyone and nothing—all at once"

"then you can disappear."

cinema

she asked
if cinema scared me
because I wish for a meaningful life;

instead, I told her
            I wish for,
sugar dappled light,
diffusing through trees;
painstaking echoes of sweetness,
on my tablecloth,
while I sip   coffee
                  or tea;

Brooklyn lassoing my ankle
with her tail
before she bites me,
and sugar dappled light
does not sweeten me,

she is one for a big screen
for owning her own property
stealing bits of life
from me

the sugar dappled light
matches me,
fades into me;

freckles on tanned skin
are cinema waiting
            for teeth

[Cinema 112 | 72703; 2022]

68

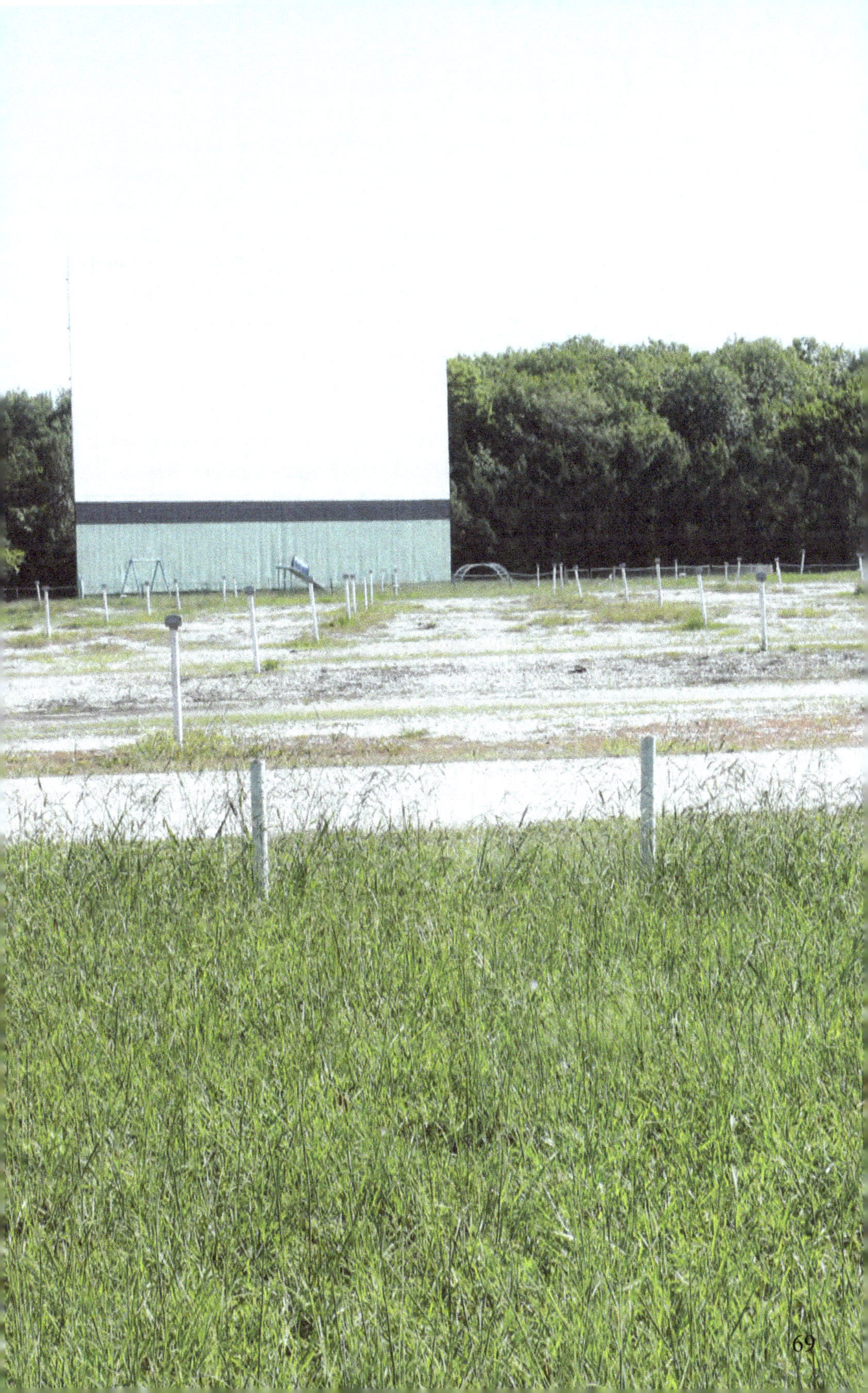

effigy

I'm sitting on a tailgate in the parking lot of a
Winn-Dixie watching candy-colored clouds
form ellipses around limbs as if
they are made for them.

        yesterday was someone's birthday who I have never met
                and I'm eating the heart out of a birthday cake
                                                Ms. Dixie made,
                while an effigy burns a hole in my pocket.

There are several thousand years to be made up for
the face of the person I might have been. She may
look the same, but I hate her just the same as I
hate me. So, I started flagging messages that use her
name—

        I'm the yin to my own yang that resonates between the
        corrugated metal in the interior of this truck bed as I
                                                watch a hustler
                                                jogging in shorts
                                                in the cold.

The only reason jogging helps clear your head is
because you've outrun your wits and have to wait
for them to catch up.

                That's why I'm glad I'm at my wits end, when
                        the owner of this truck tells me
                                to hurry the fuck up.

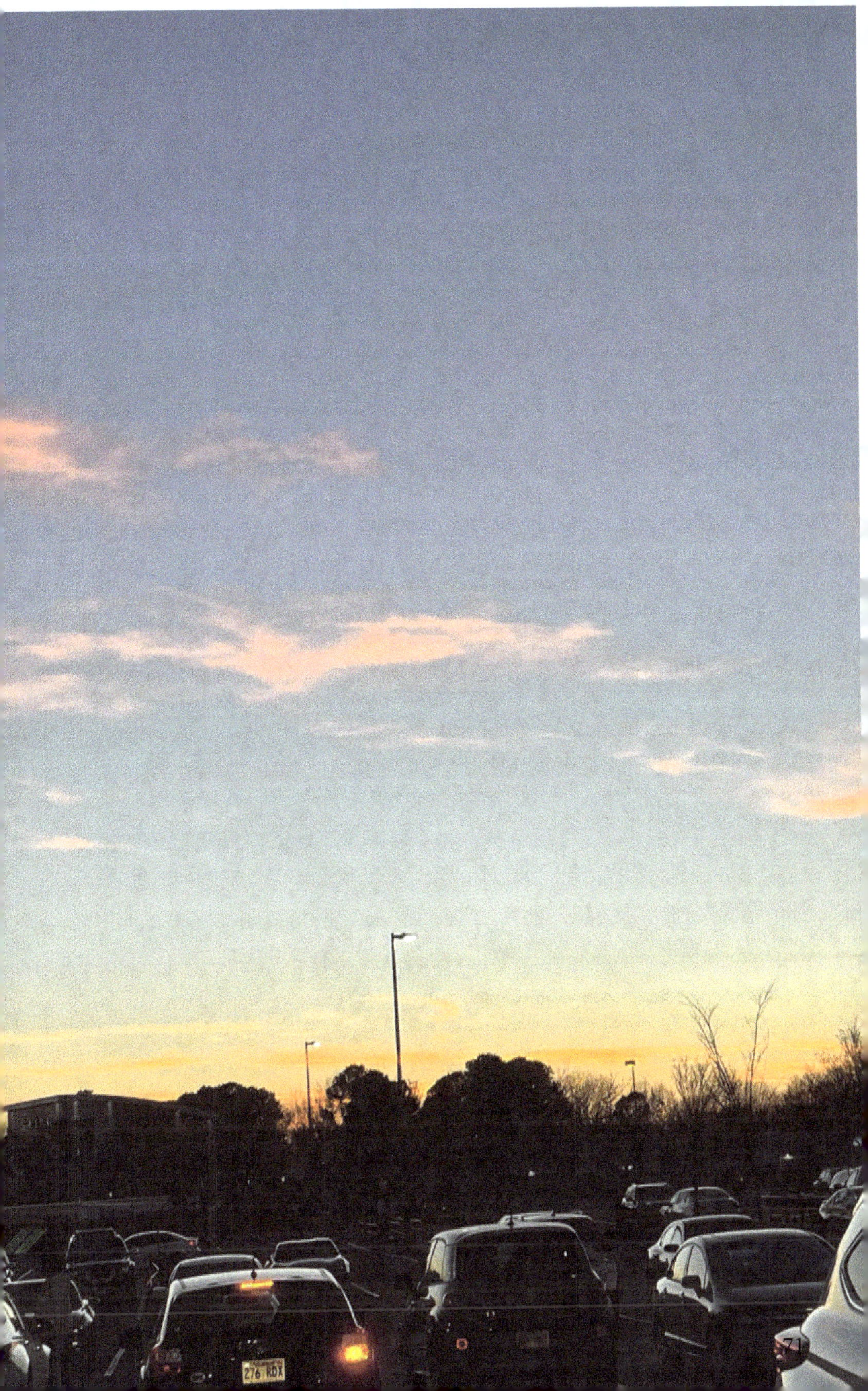

276 RDX

stuffed

Don't hate me because I'm completely ordinary looking. Hate
me because when you corner me, I'll squeeze the pulp from the
tomatoes you're throwing into a glass and pretend I needed
them to make a bloody mary before I summon her with her name
three times in front of the mirror you've been ignoring.

  If I asked you to start being who you always wanted to be—
    how long would it take for you to feel like you had been
    faking your entire life—to convince yourself, you weren't
                                      who you'd always been?

I'm out here on a limb again.

the 275 corridor bridge is building passages into my same
foreign land. Cranes carrying cargo, rest their necks
haphazardly on billows of scruffy cloud pillows,
while egrets fly like fighter pilots between them.
Their weight shifts the breeze
filtering through my window
before it starts to sound like a helicopter
womping between the seats.
                        and in that moment,

  I am no longer me nor you nor fantastical creature I dreamt
            the contour of my makeup could make me up to be.

I am still, stuffed in a black linen jacket and waiting for
the car behind me to beep.

a transition period before you hear the beeeeeep
before the receiver can hear you say, you're sorry you missed
me.

[Take Gregg; 72703; Jan 26, 2026]

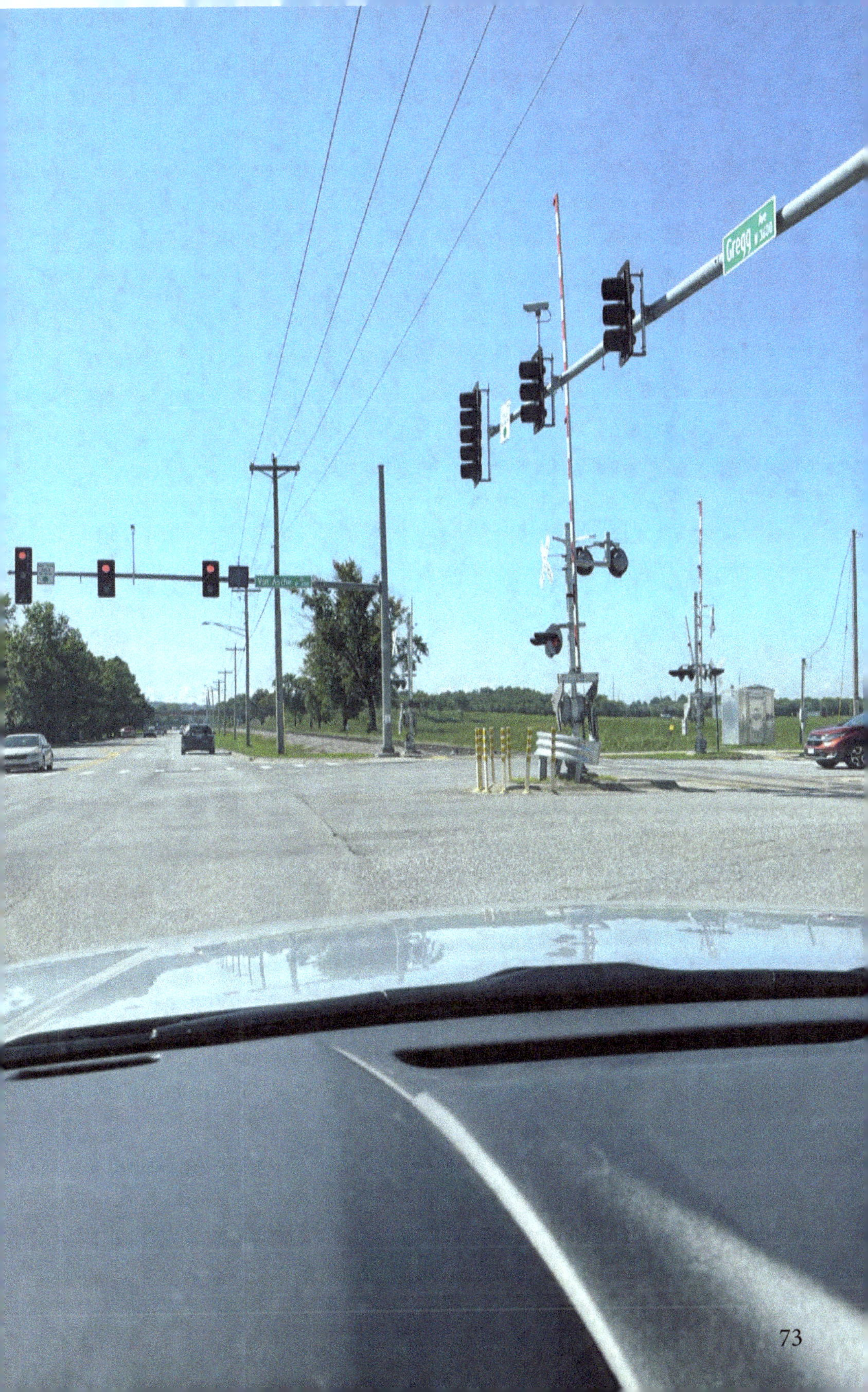
Gregg
Van Asche

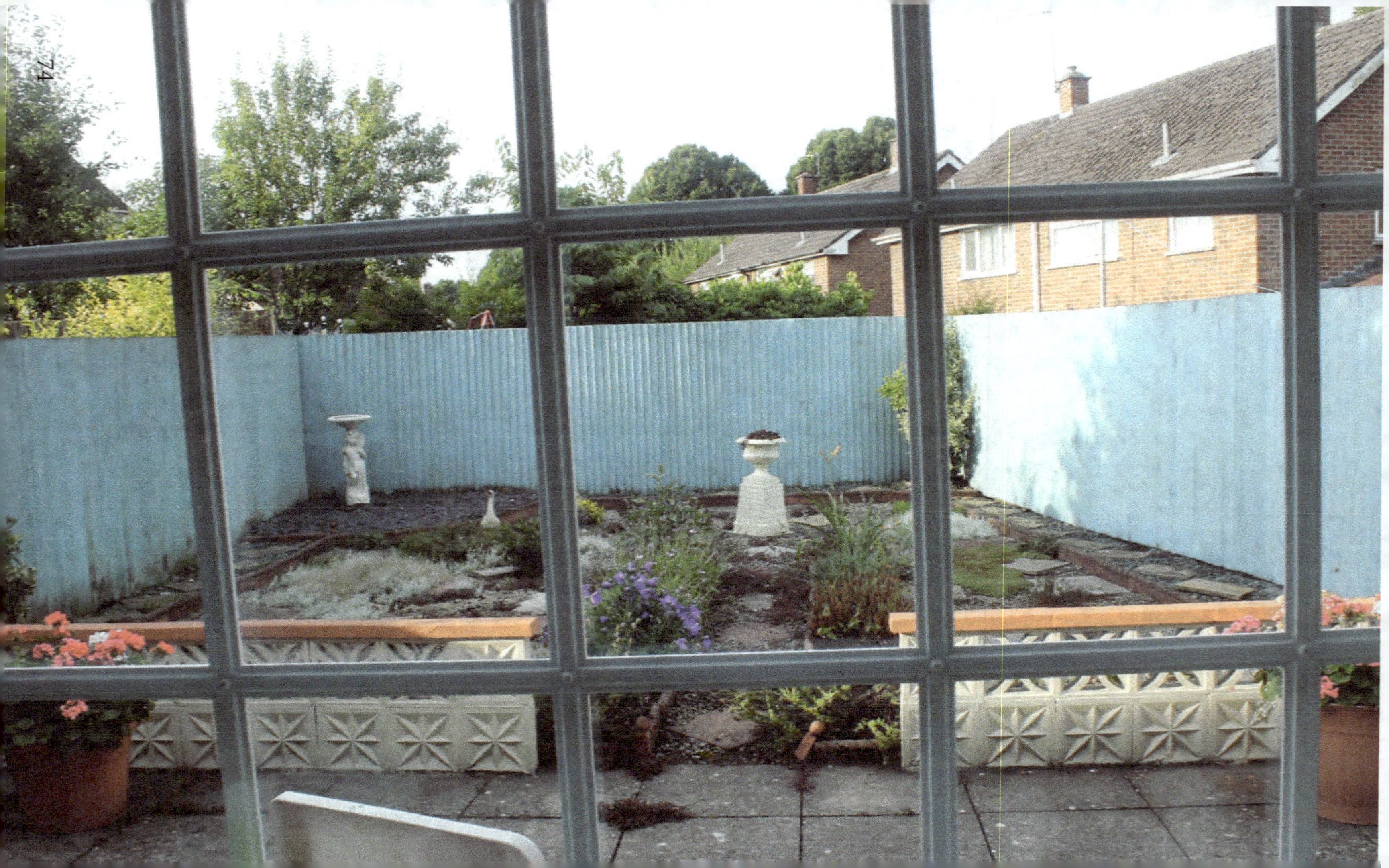

beans

Tell me what it's like to take my name
while I boil beans for breakfast.

I want you to win all the money you've bet on me, a
horse with no name, and no identity—except
mother, sister, daughter.

My assets are frozen to you.
        would you freeze them to me?

would you let my piss sit in the still of the bowl to
mix with your stream before you flush it down
arbitrarily?

        the color darkens as if to say…isn't it richer
        this way.
As I calm crisis calls for existence that yearns to fade
away, and tell them I don't know how but it will be okay.

They stare back at me— the beans.

They are sad, and had someone left them alone, could
have grown new leaves,

but I boil them down
        for you and I to eat.

six

when I was six
my mother told me   she thought of dying
she always hid her eyes when she said it
she always cast long shadows
        while she spoke softly
        about the never ending wanting

and I am my own mother

when I was six
she spoke of sippy cups
            carrying dust
because she couldn't bear the thought
of a cabinet harboring
her drinking cups
I am my own mother
when I think of drinking;

8:42 is tethered to my wrist
the check in code that says the time
                              & my name
    <my favorite flower is my name>
my mother's name
            is set   on a tag
                              on her toe
            and I am my own mother today

[an AM Strip, Anna Marie Island, February 7, 2022]

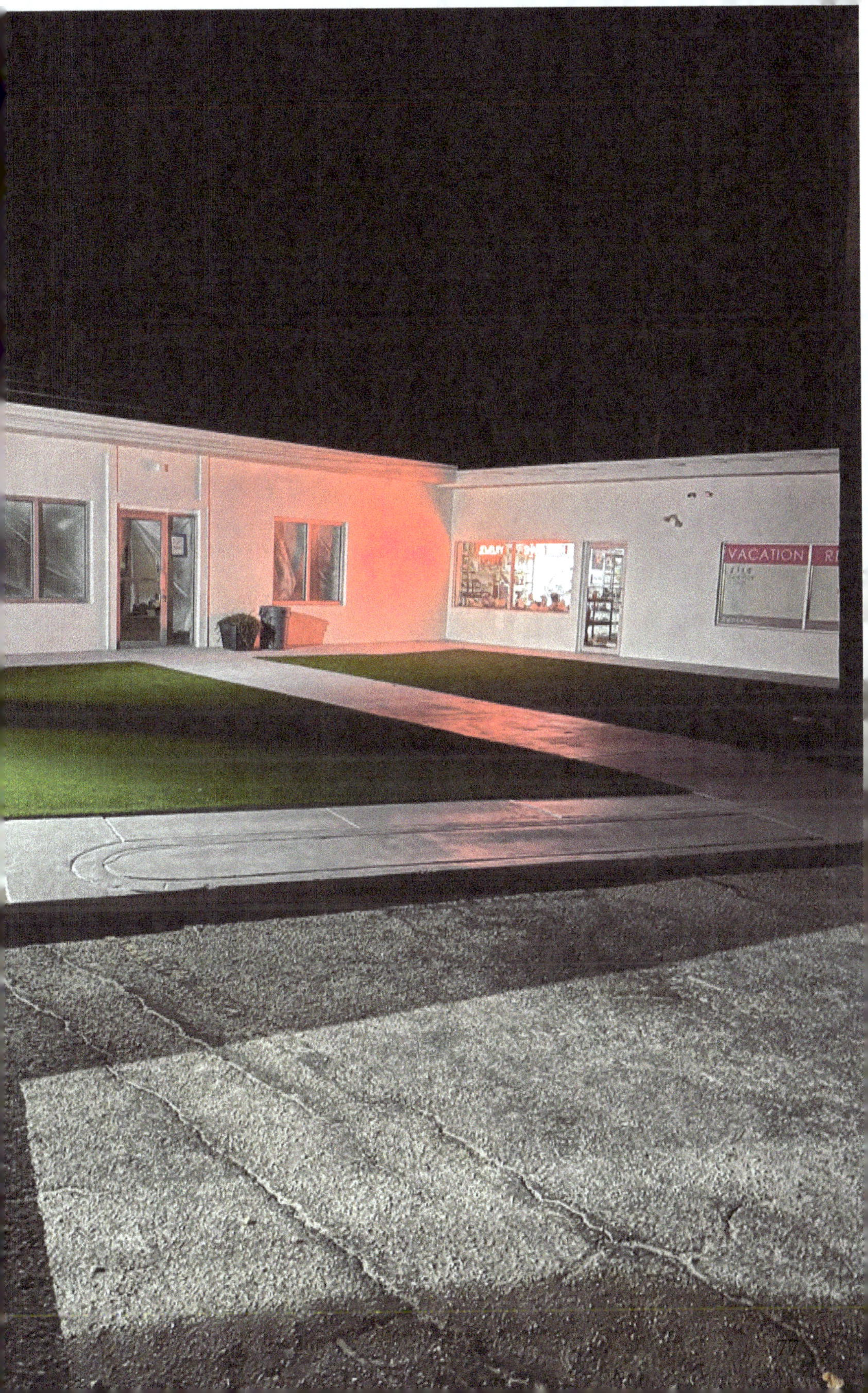
VACATION R

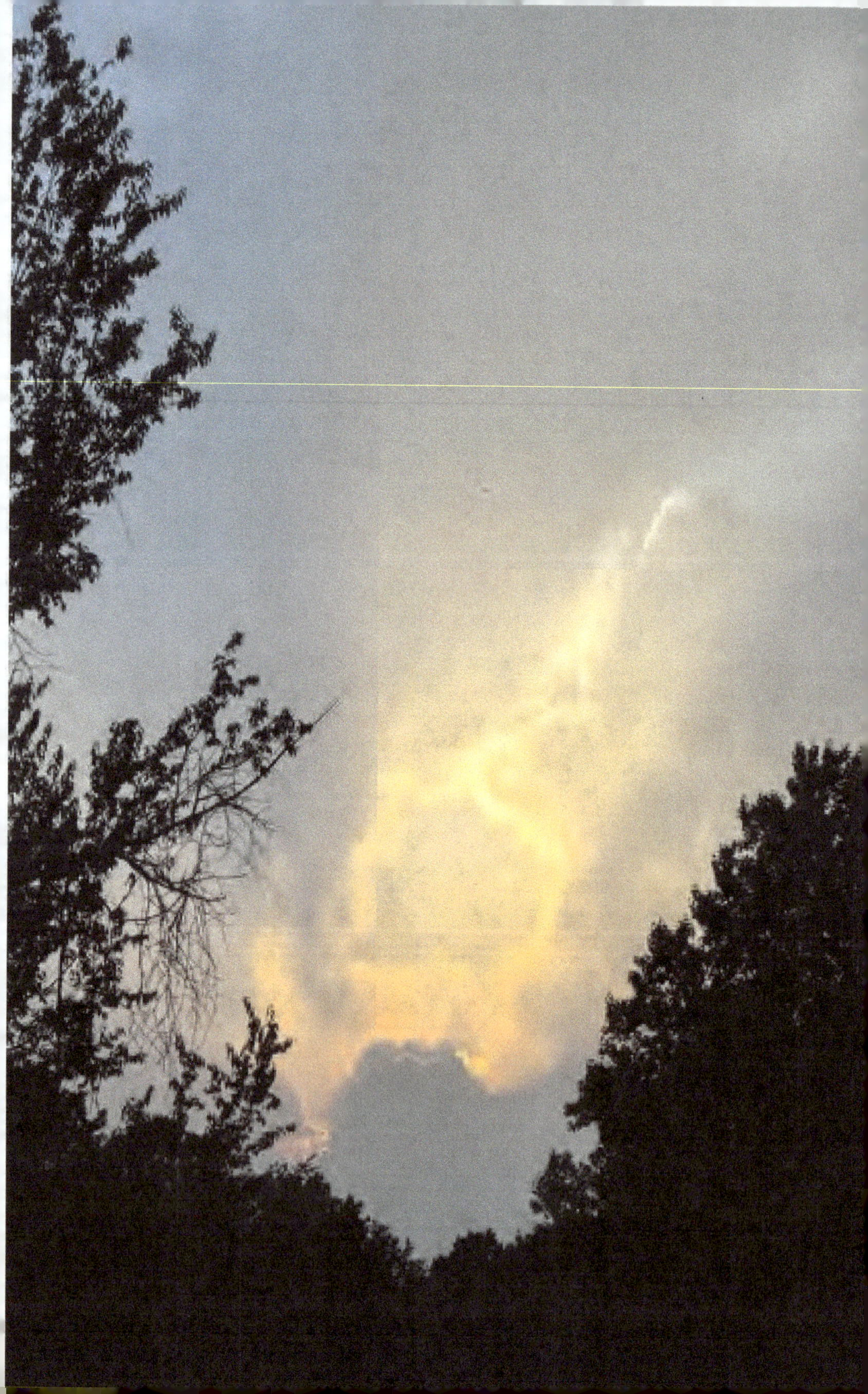

songbird

I saw a songbird
            sing your name,
before it spelled,
the ways wind could break
                            open
                            old wounds;
before,
I could gather coffee
between my lips;

I think,
there was no greater   moment
than the one, when
a stem fell across its back
            and it pretended it was dead;

I saw a songbird
      sing your name
before the wind could break it;

I saw it   moments before
      time twisted
words into stories meant for sonnets,

stories that were founded,   to a songbird fountain
where water lay,
      like gullets   by the mountains;

I saw a songbird   sing your name,
and it filled up rites of passage

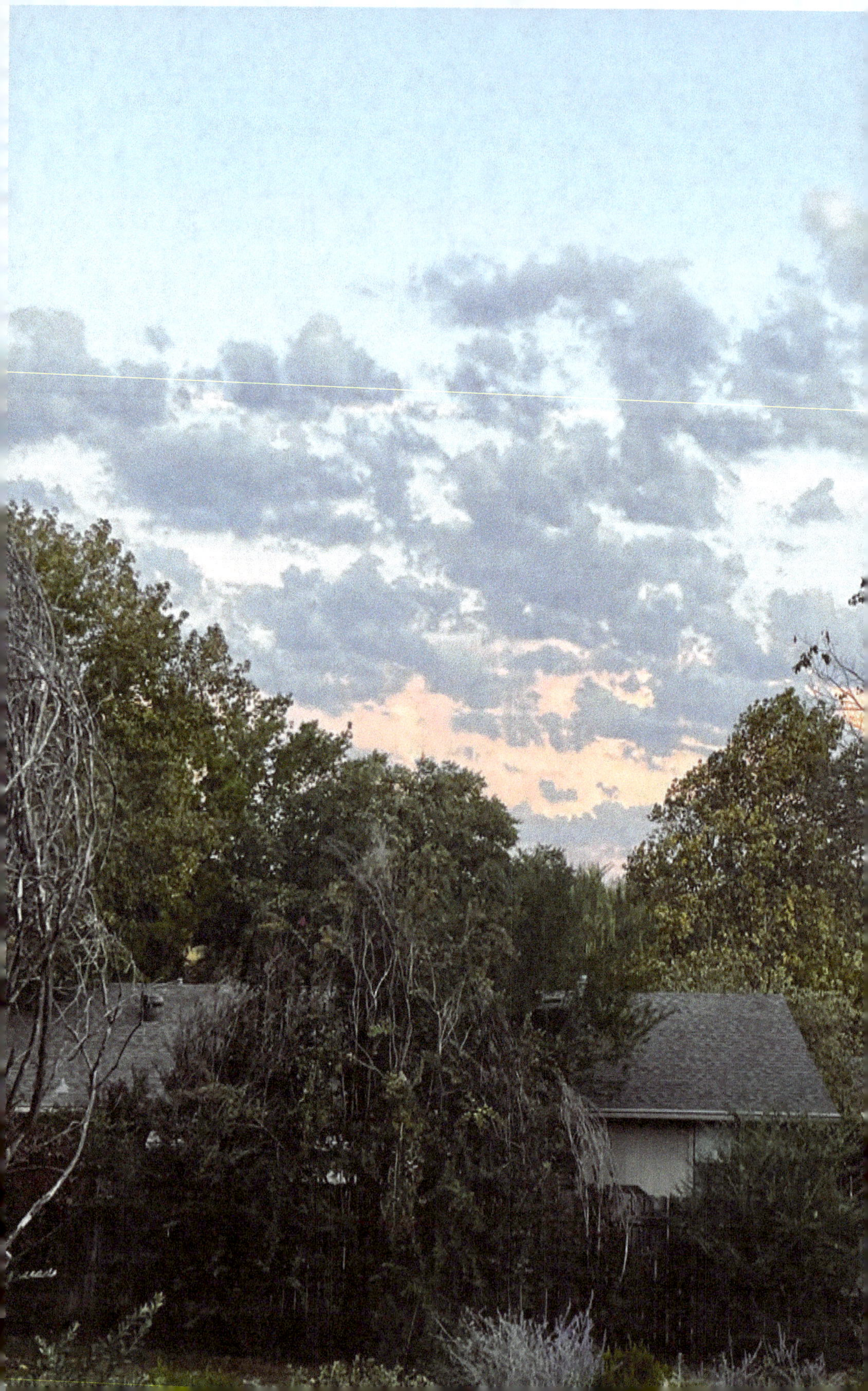

violet

soft hands laid my body,
     in a ravine;
     wrapped in muslin
          under the violet doghouse;

i think,
     i had been standing,
     wash basin staring   up at me
          palming aspirin, behind my teeth
               with a quarter,
                    colored amber,
                    feeling warmer;
i stood,   in the garden
               to feel taller,
i stood,   next to the ocean
               to feel smaller,
i stood—at the crease of my knee
               by a toilet bowl
               waiting to meet destiny;

my feet are now a few fellow feet, from
     the trough meant for pink piglet snouts
          beside the violet doghouse;
          before they search me for truffles,
     inside the blanket used,   to make me smaller;
all i wanted was to feel taller;
tales that told me
     life was not about
     who knew your father;

i wished for violets,   on my grave
          as i threw up   my quarter
               in the toilet;
instead, i got them   where the dog lives
     i hope my bones taste,
               good to him

No

tes:

No

tes:

9 798985 919523